Cynthia G. Hurley is an experienced horsewoman and co-owner and manager of Springtree, Inc. in Alachua, Florida where she trains and shows dressage horses. In addition to teaching dressage and basic horsemanship, the author has written numerous articles for riding magazines, among them *American Horseman* and *Horse, Of Course!* She is an active member of many professional organizations, including the Deep South Dressage Association, the American Horse Shows Association, and the North Florida Hunter and Jumper Association.

Doreen M. Willmeroth, also an experienced horsewoman, is a well-known professional photographer in Gainesville, Florida.

TEACH YOURSELF

Cynthia G. Hurley

Photographs by Doreen M. Willmeroth

TO RIDE
A HORSE

A SPECTRUM BOOK

PRENTICE-HALL, INC.
Englewood Cliffs, New Jersey 07632

Library of Congress Cataloging in Publication Data

HURLEY, CYNTHIA G
   Teach yourself to ride a horse.

   (A Spectrum Book)
   Includes index.
   1. Horsemanship.   I. Title.
SF309.H83   798′.23   77-22814
ISBN 0-13-896704-0
ISBN 0-13-896696-6 pbk.

Teach Yourself to Ride a Horse, by Cynthia G. Hurley

Printed in the United States of America

10   9   8   7   6   5   4   3   2   1

PRENTICE-HALL INTERNATIONAL, INC., *London*
PRENTICE-HALL OF AUSTRALIA PTY. LIMITED, *Sydney*
PRENTICE-HALL OF CANADA, LTD., *Toronto*
PRENTICE-HALL OF INDIA PRIVATE LIMITED, *New Delhi*
PRENTICE-HALL OF JAPAN, INC., *Tokyo*
PRENTICE-HALL OF SOUTHEAST ASIA PTE. LTD., *Singapore*
WHITEHALL BOOKS LIMITED, *Wellington, New Zealand*

Preface

If you are a beginning or intermediate rider, this book is for you. We cover basic horsemanship in sixteen clear, easy-to-follow lessons. You will learn everything, from selecting your horse through such advanced topics as jumping over fences in horse shows and playing Western games on horseback. Each new technique is explained clearly, in detail, and illustrated with diagrams and photographs. We even include tests and form quizzes to help you judge your knowledge and progress.

You may not be able to afford to pay a qualified instructor for riding lessons. You may prefer to practice new skills on your own. This text is for you. In addition, riding schools and teachers will find this manual a valuable aid for their riding pupils. The student can read about riding theory and look at pictures of riders before trying new techniques at the school.

Huntseat, saddleseat, and Western horsemanship are covered. All three styles of riding are introduced through balance seat, the most modern way of riding. The balance seat rider is secure in the saddle, comfortable, and in control of his horse. He can easily go on to advanced horsemanship and dressage, if he so desires.

The author and photographer are available to answer questions, to help in setting up a riding program for a school or group of individuals, or to give short clinics with this manual. You may get in touch by writing to: *Cynthia G. Hurley, c/o Springtree Inc., Rt. 1, Box 321A, Alachua, Florida 32615.*

Doreen and I wish to thank the following people for their invaluable aid in making this book possible: Ms. Lynne A. Lumsden, Ms. Dorothy Werner, and Ms. Claudia Citarella of Prentice-Hall; Mr. Bart Lewis of Reflections Photography; Colonel V. A. von Alenitch; and my husband, Drew Hurley.

Contents

IV
IN THE
OPEN

8
Problems with Your Horse in the Open   255

1

BASIC INFOR-MATION

Before you begin to ride, you should be familiar with certain terms of the language of horsemanship. Unless you have some idea of the meaning of these words, you will be unable to get full value from the lessons. In Chapter 1, I discuss the necessary words briefly, with illustrations to help you understand and remember them. At the end of this section is a simple test that can help you study.

In order to follow this book with the greatest success, you will need certain items. First among the necessities is a good horse. In Chapter 1, I go over how to select your mount. Included are several guides and check-lists that you should use when you carry out your search.

Chapter 2 mentions clothing for you (you should dress well for better comfort) and some necessary learning aids. If these aids are not readily available, you can make them according to the plans provided.

1 Knowing and Choosing Your Horse

PARTS OF THE HORSE

You must have a good mount for your lessons. A good horse can help you become a good rider: a difficult horse might give you so much trouble that you give up riding completely! I will go over good and bad characteristics of horses in this chapter. You can learn a lot by studying what I say. However, it takes years of experience to really learn how to select horses. You will do best if you have someone help you choose your mount. This person can be a professional horseman, or he can be a friend who knows horses. Whoever it is, please do not trust a horse seller! Remember, if someone wants to sell you a horse, he has his own interests in mind. Get someone to help you who will have your interests in mind. Then, you will be more likely to find a horse that you will like, and that will give you a comfortable and safe ride.

You should study the parts of the horse in order to become familiar with the terms. These terms will be used later on in this book, and you may have trouble following the text if you have not learned them. Below, I give you a list of the terms for each part of the horse, as well as a brief description of desirable and undesirable traits. The actual location of the part on the horse's anatomy is shown in Figure 1-1.

3

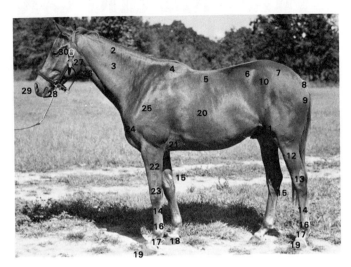

Figure 1–1. Parts of the horse: (1) poll; (2) crest; (3) neck; (4) withers; (5) back; (6) loins; (7) croup; (8) tail; (9) point of the rump; (10) point of the hip; (11) stifle; (12) gaskin; (13) hock; (14) cannon; (15) chestnut; (16) fetlock; (17) pastern; (18) coronet; (19) hoof; (20) barrel; (21) heart; (22) forearm; (23) knee; (24) point of the shoulder; (25) shoulder; (26) throttle; (27) jaw; (28) chin and lips; (29) nostril; (30) eye.

Poll (1). Sometimes horses get serious boils between their ears which is known as "poll evil." If the poll has open cuts or weepy wounds, do not select this horse for your mount.

Crest (2). The curve on the horse's neck. Not all horses have crests. Some have straight necks. Others have ewe necks, where the top-line of the neck is actually concave (the opposite of a crest). Straight necks are all right; but ewe necks are considered a fault, as ewe-necked horses seldom make safe or comfortable mounts.

Neck (3). Necks can be too thick or too thin. Thick-necked horses tend to pull against the bit, making them hard to control. Thin-necked horses tend to carry their heads too high or too low, due to the weakness of the neck muscles. Later in this book we will discuss the balance in the horse. You can flip forward to this section if you want to see how the ideal neck should look.

Withers (4). The withers, or high point of the horse's back, are the anchor for many important muscles in the horse's back and neck. Therefore, well-shaped withers are important in determining what a horse will be able to do. The withers should be medium to high: You should be able to see them clearly. The region should be long, extending into the neck and the back. However, if the withers are too high and thin, you may have trouble finding a saddle that will fit your horse.

Back (5). A good back is medium to short in length, and straight. Sway backs (concave) are weak. Roached backs (convex) are strong, but unattractive. If the backbone is visible, the horse is too thin.

Loins (6). The loins extend from the last rib to the croup. Good loins are short and broad. Long loins greatly weaken the carrying capacity of the horse.

Croup (7). The croup should be long, and gently sloped. Commonly, croups are too flat, bringing the hind legs out behind the body or too short and sloping, making the horse weaker because the hind legs are too far under the body.

Tail (8). The tail should be full, and free of lice and mange. Lice are about ¼ inch long, and plainly visible to the eye. With mange, or with fungus, the skin will be discolored, and the hair will fall out, however, fungus is curable with medicine. Sometimes horses get tumors on the tail, which may be cancerous. The best thing for you to do is to examine the horse carefully. If you see any lumps or bald spots, get a veterinarian to examine them before you make your selection. You would not want to ride a horse with cancer or mange.

Point of the rump (9). The points should be thick and well muscled. You should see no bone. Also, both points, right and left, should be at the same height. Sometimes horses are injured by blows, causing a deformity to the point of the rump on one side of the body.

Point of the hip (10). Again, both points should be the same height. The point of the hip should not be too visible. Prominent points indicate thinness or coarse breeding.

Stifle (11). In the anatomy of skeletons, the stifle of the horse corresponds to the knee of the human. The stifle should be thick and well-muscled.

Gaskin (12). The gaskin, which goes from the stifle to the hock, should have muscles both inside and out. Many horses don't have enough muscle on the inside of the gaskin.

Hock (13). The hock in the horse corresponds to the ankle in the human. The hock should be large and free from swellings, and both hocks should be the same shape. When the horse is standing square, with all four legs under his body, the hock should line up perpendicularly with the point of the rump. If the hock is too far under the body, or too far behind the body, the horse will be predisposed to lameness.

Fetlock (14). The fetlock on each leg should be flat and large. It should be free from hard and soft swellings. All the fetlocks should look basically the same. The fetlock is frequently called the ankle, although it has no correspondence in anatomy to the human ankle.

Chestnut (15). Chestnuts are callouses on the inside of each leg. They are inherited in all horses, and have no known function.

Cannon (16). Cannons on both hind and front legs should be large and flat, with well-defined tendons. The cannon should be the same width from the hock, or knee, to the fetlock (ankle). If the cannon is broader near the fetlock, it is a sign either of a weakness in the animal's structure, or of an injury, such as a bowed tendon.

Pastern (17). The pastern should be fairly long and slope with a 40 to 45 degree angle. If the pastern is too straight or short, the horse will have rough, uncomfortable, choppy gaits (way of going). If the pastern is too long or sloping, the horse will ride smoothly, but will lack strength in his legs.

Coronet (18). The coronet corresponds to the cuticle in the human. It secretes the wall of the hoof. Any deep cuts or tears in the coronet will cause a permanent deformity in the hoof wall. Sometimes a blow to the coronet will cause a temporary stop in the function of a small section of the hoof-secreting cells. Later, the hoof will show evidence of what happened by the appearance of a small hole in the hoof wall which will gradually grow down the hoof until it reaches the bottom. These holes are usually not serious. You should ask a good farrier, or horseshoer, before you select a horse. He will advise you if the horse has any serious problems with his feet.

Hoof (19). The hoof corresponds to the fingernail and last bone in a human finger or toe. The horse's hoof should be medium sized—large enough to support his weight, but not large enough to make him clumsy. Many horses have trouble with their feet. There is an old saying "No foot, no horse," this saying is unfortunately very true. If your horse has cracked, split hooves, he might go lame. You cannot do much riding on a lame horse! Also, shoes are not always the answer; shoes will keep the hooves from cracking only if they stay on the feet. Many times the horse's hooves will split around the nails that hold the shoes in place, if this happens, the shoes will not stay on. Before you select a horse, it is a good idea to pay special attention to his feet. Remember black hooves are the hardest, and are less likely to crack or split. The striped hooves of an appaloosa horse are also very tough. Gray hooves (many chestnut horses have them) are next in hardness, while white hooves are the softest. The color of a horse's feet should not be the only reason you select or reject him for your mount. You should simply bear in mind that if your horse has soft feet, you will have higher farrier bills. Ask a good farrier to check out your horse's feet before you commit yourself to taking your lessons on him. Of course, this is much more important if you buy the horse. If you rent him, the hooves are someone else's problem. I'll talk in more detail about the advantages and disadvantages of buying or renting a horse later.

Barrel (20). The barrel refers to the body of the horse from the front to the hind legs. A horse should be both thick and deep in the barrel. If the horse is narrow, he will have little endurance. If the horse is shallow or narrow in the back part of the barrel, through the belly, he will be a big eater, and hard to keep fat. A horse can also be too big in the belly. This is usually due to fat, but it can be caused by pregnancy. You might suspect that a fat mare is pregnant, especially if there is any chance at all that she has been around a stallion.

Heart (21). The heart is also called the girth. This is where the girth or cinch of the saddle will be fastened. Generally, the deeper a horse is through the heart, the more endurance he will have. This is because the deeper girth leads to better breathing and more lung capacity.

Forearm (22). The horse's forearm corresponds to the forearm of a human. It should be fairly long and well-muscled.

Knee (23). The knee of the horse should be large and flat. It corresponds with the wrist in the human. Knees are susceptible to injury; therefore the knee should look sturdy, and it should neither buckle forward (buck knees) nor bend backwards (calf knees).

Point of the shoulder (24). This should be thick, deep, and well-muscled.

Shoulder (25). The shoulder should be long, and slope at about a 40–45 degree angle. If the shoulder is too straight, the horse will take short, choppy, uncomfortable strides. A shoulder that is too short indicates a general lack of sturdiness throughout the horse's entire body.

Throttle (26). Also called a throat latch, the throttle is the portion of the horse's neck directly behind the jaws. If you can see no definite throttle on a horse, it indicates that the horse will be unable to carry his head correctly. The horse should bend, or flex his neck at the poll, an action that causes a bend in the throttle. However, a short or non-existent throttle will not bend; rather, it will pinch, thus cutting off the horse's breathing. A horse with a neck like this will always carry his head straight out in front of him.

Jaw (27). The jaw should be large and flat. The space between the jaws should be wide, in order to allow for the passage of air and food from the horse's head to his neck.

Chin and lips (28). The chin and lips should be free of injuries and deformities. A horse with a very thick chin and lips will frequently be a puller, and hard to control under saddle. This is due to the reduced sensitivity of the mouth.

Nostril (29). A horse should have wide nostrils that will allow for the intake of large volumes of air.

Eye (30). The eye of the horse is usually brown, but it may be white or blue. The pupil is dark blue and rectangular in shape. If the horse's eye is large and bulging, he may be flighty, due to faulty vision. If the eyes are small and set deep in the head, the horse may be stubborn for the same reason.

COLOR AND MARKINGS

The most common horse colors—and there are many variations—are as follows:

Black. Black all over. A true black has no brown hairs, not even on his muzzle.

Seal Brown. May be mostly black, but will have brown on the muzzle, and usually on the flank. A brown usually has darker brown, but not black, legs, mane, and tail.

Bay. Any shade of brown or chestnut with black mane and tail, and with black on the lower extremities of the legs.

Chestnut. The animal is basically the same color all over, though the mane and tail may be lighter or darker. Ranges in shade from very dark—nearly black—to light red or orange. The lightest chestnuts are also called sorrels.

Dun. Duns are dusty yellow to bright yellow in color. Some may be blue-gray or mouse colored. Frequently they have darker legs, mane, and tail, and a stripe down their backs.

Buckskin. A yellow colored horse with a true black mane and tail, and black on the extremities of the legs.

Palomino. A yellow or gold horse with a white mane and tail.

Cream. A cream ranges in color from very light palomino to almost white. Frequently they will show light palomino markings in the early spring, only to turn nearly white by fall due to the bleaching action of the sun.

Grey. A grey animal is born some other color, such as brown or chestnut. As it ages, white hairs gradually take over, so that the animal whitens with age. Some greys are white by the age of four; others never turn completely white.

White. A true white horse is born white and never shows palomino markings.

Roan. Roan is a mixture of white hairs and colored hairs. Roan horses are born roan, and do not lighten with age. Sometimes a horse which is greying will look roan.

Pinto. A black and white, or brown and white, or brown, black, and white horse—sometimes called a paint. You will see large areas of white on the animal's body. Pintos may have each eye a different color. For example, one eye may be brown, and the other eye white or blue. This does not indicate blindness in the blue or white eye.

Appaloosa. These are spotted horses in many different color and spot patterns. Frequently an appaloosa's coat pattern will change slightly every spring and fall. Appaloosas always have striped hooves, mottled skin, and considerable white showing around a dark iris and pupil in the eye.

CHOOSING YOUR HORSE

Sources of Supply

RENT

Many areas have hack stables where you can rent horses and tack by the hour. If you decide to rent your mount, be sure to visit several stables before you decide to use one in particular. The stable you choose should be clean—not resembling the local dump—with healthy, fat, calm horses, and a good riding ring. The tack should be clean and in good repair. You should be able to arrange to have the *same* horse every day, and to use the *same* saddle. The saddle should fit you. The advantages of renting from a hack stable include the following: (1) You won't be required to care for the horse, and it will probably be saddled and waiting for you when you arrive; (2) you will have a choice of horses; (3) other people will be around in case you need help. The disadvantages are as follows: (1) The horses are ridden by a lot of people, and yours may be tired or soured when you come to ride; (2) you cannot expect to have the ring to yourself, since other customers will be competing with you for space; (3) the stable will probably be closed on certain days, and you may not always be able to ride when you want to or when you have free time.

BORROW

You may have a friend who will let you borrow his or her horse and tack. This arrangement can work if the horse is suitable for you, and if you are willing to do your share in the care and maintenance of the animal. Even if you are not asked, you should volunteer to clean tack, to help around the stable, and to help out with the feed and farrier bills. Advantages of borrowing a horse include: (1) Only a few people are riding the animal, so that he will probably be fresh and eager when you take your lesson; (2) you will probably be able to ride more often for less cost. Disadvantages include: (1) You must ride at the convenience of your friend, who may want the horse for other purposes when you come, or may simply tire of having you around; (2) the horse may not be suitable for you, yet you'll have no other choice; (3) the tack may not fit you, and again, you'll have no choice of tack; (4) the facilities may not be complete. You cannot, after all, ask your friend to build things for your use.

BUY

If you own land, or live near a boarding stable, you may decide to buy a horse. Many people are happiest with their own horse. They see the animal in the stable as well as in the ring, and thus get to know the horse a lot better. Knowledge builds confidence. The advantages of buying a horse include: (1) You don't have to share your horse with others, and you can get an animal, and tack, suited to your needs; (2) you have a chance of getting some of your money back should you give up riding. Disadvantages include: (1) The initial investment is much more—it will run from hundreds to thousands of dollars; (2) you must pay all the upkeep, which can be high if you must pay board; (3) you must take care of the horse yourself or pay another to do it for you; (4) you must either build all your own facilities, or find a boarding stable that has the facilities.

One note of caution: never buy any horse unless he has been approved by a veterinarian, a farrier, and a friend or professional who is a good rider. These people will check the horse's soundness and suitability. Remember, the horse may only cost a few hundred dollars, but your life is priceless. As you are going to be riding, and trusting your life and health to this animal, you dare not risk buying a lemon.

Characteristics of a Good School Horse

No matter how you acquire your mount (rent, borrow, or buy), he must have certain characteristics in order to be a suitable mount for your beginning lessons. Later on, when you become an experienced rider, you will be able to ride different types of horses. For now, however, you need an absolutely fool-proof mount. You need an animal which is so gentle and well trained that he will never place your safety in jeopardy. You will be much happier with the horse if he is sound, healthy, and well mannered as well. Following is a brief description of the characteristics of a good beginner's mount.

SIZE

The size of a horse is measured in hands; a hand is four inches. The height of the horse is measured from the highest point of his withers to the ground.

Horses come in many different sizes. Unless you have a personal lackey to hoist you aboard, you will probably be happier at first with a small to medium sized animal. Smaller horses are easier to mount, and you will probably find that mounting is a problem at first. It takes a while to develop the muscles used in ascending to the saddle. You can use two tests to tell if the horse you are considering is a good size for you. First, stand beside the horse and lay your arm over his back (see Figure 1–2). If you can do this easily, without standing on your toes or bending over, the horse is in your range, and it will be relatively easy for you to spring (or climb) aboard. The second test is a test of the barrel size of the horse, to see how it fits the length of your legs. Different heights in horses have little relationship to widths: Tall horses may be very narrow, and short horses may be very broad. Ideally, if you are sitting on a horse with your legs in a relaxed position, your heels should be even with the bottom of the horse's belly. If your legs end far up the side of the horse, or if they fall far past the horse's bottom line (bottom of the chest and belly), you will not be comfortable riding him. You will also

Figure 1–2. The horse is a good size for you if you can easily lay your arm over his back. Larger animals will be difficult for you to mount without help.

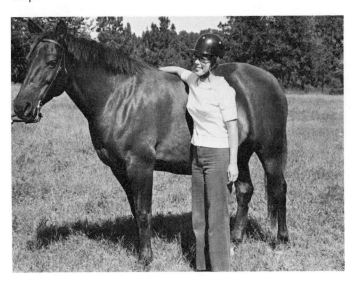

have more trouble developing a secure seat (learning to stay on without bouncing) on such an animal. Have someone help you on the animal bareback briefly to check this element of size.

SEX

Horses come in three sexes: mare (female); stallion or stud (uncastrated male), and gelding (castrated male). Sometimes horses are also sexed as filly (a mare less than five years old) or colt (a stallion or gelding less than five years old). You will want to learn on a mare or a gelding. Do not plan to learn to ride on a stallion. Even the gentlest studs tend to be aggressive and unpredictable; they are not safe mounts for beginners. Geldings are usually more stable than mares. For this reason, many people prefer them, especially as mounts for novice riders. Mares tend to be flighty when they come into heat, which is every eighteen days during the spring and summer. However, I have used many mares in teaching beginners with no trouble at all. (Incidently, it is by no means true that all geldings are sedate and even tempered.) Do not buy a colt or a filly. These animals are too young for your purposes.

AGE

The best age for a horse to learn on is over eight and under twenty years of age. If you are buying a horse, probably a ten or twelve year old is the best buy. Horses younger than eight lack the patience and experience needed to tolerate beginners' frequent mistakes. Even the gentlest young horse will sometimes become distressed and confused during the lessons. But when an animal is eight or ten years old, he is better able to shrug off our unconscious abuse. Keep in mind that horses are near the end of their active life at twenty. Even healthy looking old horses may be near-sighted or arthritic. I wouldn't buy a really old horse, but you might take lessons on one if you are offered his services.

A note of caution when you go to buy a horse: All horses

that are for sale tend to be called "seven year olds." Never believe what the owner tells you! I know of a so-called "eight-year-old" horse which turned out to be twenty-five! The buyer found out only after it was too late. Always have a good horse-veterinarian check the horse's age before you buy.

STABLE MANNERS

If you are renting a horse, his stable manners are not important to you. You won't need to handle him aside from riding. However, if you must take care of the horse, his stable manners can make all the difference in the world. Stable manners is how the horse behaves in the barn. If he has good stable manners he is calm, cooperative, and pleasant. He never bites or kicks. He is easy to groom, easy to saddle and bridle, and in general, easy to handle. Before you buy, always check the horse's stable manners. You can do this, to a great extent, by yourself. It is a good idea to put the animal through the following test:

1. Ask to see the horse in a cross-tie, if one is available. When a horse is in a cross-tie, he has a rope snapped to either side of his halter. Thus, he has a rope running from the right side of his head to a pole or wall on his righthand side, and he has a rope running from the left side of his head to a post or wall on his lefthand side. The horse can move forwards and backwards a little. He can swing his hind end back and forth, but he cannot move his head from side to side. The cross-tie is a good way to restrain a horse for grooming or saddling. You can move all around the animal, and he cannot squeeze you against a wall or fence. He should stand quietly. Does he fidget a lot or try to break loose?

2. Ask to see the horse tied to a post or rail. Leave him for at least fifteen minutes. He should stand quietly. Does he pull backwards or fidget?

3. Watch the horse being saddled. Ask that he be saddled while he is tied, as that is probably how you will do it. He should stand quietly. Does he jump about, or try to kick or bite?

4. Watch him being bridled. The horse should lower his head and open his mouth for the bit. Does he resist so that a person your size cannot bridle him without help?

5. Take a brush and brush the horse. Is he ticklish? Does he flinch away when you touch him? Does he try to kick or bite?

6. Pick up each hoof. The horse should let you hold each foot for 30 seconds or more. Does he resist your raising his hooves? Does he fight or lean once the foot is up?

7. Lead him around. Does he drag his feet or try to rush ahead? Ask to watch when he is put back in his stall or turned out to pasture. Does he try to pull away before his halter is removed?

8. If possible, watch him being caught from the pasture. Do they need to chase him, or do they need a bucket of feed to catch him?

9. Look in his stall. Is the bed dug up or stirred around? This indicates nervousness. Does it look like he's been chewing the boards? This is a bad habit.

10. How does the animal act around other horses? Is he nervous or excited? Is he sullen; does he try to kick or bite?

The more affirmative answers you have to these questions, the less you should want to buy the horse. One bad habit may be forgiven if the horse is otherwise perfect. Two bad habits, however, will be hard to live around; and three should be cause enough to reject the animal.

TRAINING

You cannot check a horse's training yourself. You must rely on a good rider to test the horse for you. However, if you watch the horse being ridden, you can tell several important things:

1. The animal should move quietly on a loose rein at walk, trot, and canter. He should neither speed up nor slow down.

2. He should be quiet even if the rider moves around a lot on his back. Have your friend try some of the exercises described later in this book. (See Lessons 1 and 3, Chapter 6 and Lesson 5, Chapter 7.)

3. He should carry his head well, both on a loose rein, and—for English-style riding—on contact. He should be neither above nor behind the bit (see Figures 1-3 and 1-4). He should move with a relaxed head and neck on loose reins at the walk, trot, and canter. He

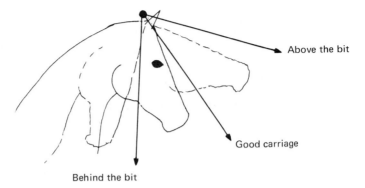

Figure 1–3. Head carriage.

shouldn't try to pull or rush forward, even if his rider does a lot of bouncing around (see Figure 1-4).

4. If you plan to learn to jump, your mount should have some jumping experience. He should go over a low jump (18-24 inches) under a rider, and without speeding up, on a loose rein at the walk and the trot.

Figure 1–4. Anrock illustrates relaxation at a slow trot. His rider has her heels up and is bouncing in the saddle, but he doesn't seem to care.

APPEARANCE AND BALANCE

The appearance of the horse you ride is not really important, except as appearance relates to soundness and to the abilities of the animal. Many people make the mistake of buying a horse because they think he's beautiful, because they like his color, or because they think he looks impressive. All these factors are valid reasons to choose a mount, IF the horse is otherwise suitable for you! Unless you have unlimited money to spend, you will probably have to compromise in some area. Remember, it is better to buy an unattractive horse which is otherwise suitable than to buy a beautiful horse that lacks the calmness or training you need. Later, when you have experience riding, you can always sell the plain animal and buy one with a little more class.

Several aspects of balance in the horse relate directly to the agility and ease of handling of your mount. I have diagrammed these aspects in Figures 1–5a & b. They are explained below:

1. The distance from the middle point in the withers to the tip of the muzzle should be the same, or longer, than the distance from the middle point of the withers to the end of the meaty portion of the tail.

2. The head should be about the same length as the distance from the highest point of the withers to the point of the shoulder.

3. The line from the elbow to the stifle should be about one-third longer than the line from the end of the withers to the beginning of the croup.

4. The forelegs should be about the same length as the depth from the highest point of the withers to the lowest point of the heart.

5. The legs should be well placed and stand squarely under the body.

FEET

The old saying, "No foot, no horse," means that no animal, no matter how perfect otherwise, is useful or valuable if he has bad feet. A horse cannot stay sound on sore or flat feet any more

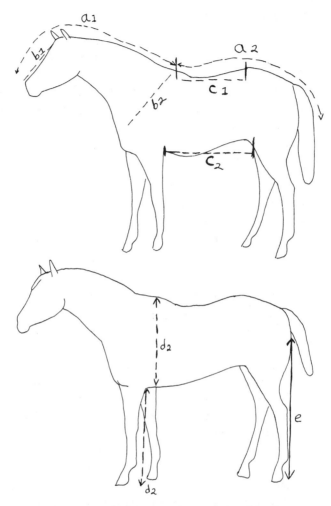

Figure 1-5a,b. Balance in the horse: a1 should be equal to or greater than a2; b1 should be equal to or less than b2; c1 should be one-third less than c2; d1 should be equal to d2; at e, the point of the hock should be even with the point of the rump when the horse stands with all four legs squarely under his body.

than a person can. If you are buying a horse, it is always wise to check the feet first. Until you become really familiar with the good and bad points, and how to look for them, you should have a farrier give you his opinion before you purchase any animal. Some of the faults that may be present follow:

Flat soles. This is very common in horses. The soles of the hoof should be cupped. If they are flat, the animal will be susceptible to bruised soles and sore feet. Sometimes this fault can be compensated for with shoes.

Shallow feet. Reject a horse with shallow feet (very thin hooves and low heels; ask your friend or a farrier to check his feet if you are not sure they are deep enough), particularly if he also has flat soles. This animal will have all the problems of a horse with flat soles, as well as tendencies towards more serious lamenesses.

Cracked hoof wall. Cracks are not serious unless the animal is lame. If the horse is lame from a crack, the crack is deep and will be very expensive to treat and difficult to cure. If the horse is not lame, a good trimming, hoof dressing, and perhaps shoes, will probably correct the problem. Be sure to ask the farrier about it.

Long, narrow feet. A horse with feet like this will probably have a tendency to stumble. The front hooves should be round, the back hooves oval.

Founder, or laminitis. This is a disease caused by a variety of factors—usually over-feeding or poor management, although disease and high fever can also be the cause. The condition attacks the hooves, and results in misshapen hooves, and, sometimes, permanent lameness. Although the condition can be corrected in many cases by special shoeing, the cure is long and expensive. Also, once founder has attacked, it tends to recur. Don't buy a horse which is foundered. Ask your farrier or vet if you are not sure. The symptoms are large, extremely visible rings around the hoof; long, upturned toes—frequently

Figure 1–6. Parts of the hoof: (1) frog; (2) cleft; (3) bars; (4) sole; (5) wall; (6) heel; (7) quarters; (8) toe.

with splits between the hoof wall and the sole—and lameness (not always present).

Other lameness. Sometimes a horse is lame for no apparent reason. You may look at a horse which has a so-called "fake limp." This means either that the owner doesn't know what is causing the lameness, or that he doesn't want you to know. Personally, I believe that horses are not intelligent enough to fake a limp. However, even if the limp were faked, the horse is still useless for your purposes. A limp is a limp, no matter what the cause. A frequent cause of "faked limps" is navicular disease—a break of the navicular bone in the hoof. There is no permanent cure for this problem, though veterinarians sometimes cut the nerves that lead to the navicular bone so that the horse feels no pain and goes sound, or does not limp. Eventually, however, the animal will go lame again.

Thrush. This is a fungus infection of the frog and sole of the hoof. The frog is the fleshy, sensitive part of the horse's hoof. A horse with thrush will become lame because his feet are sore and hurt. Usually thrush is caused by damp, unsanitary conditions. Like all fungal infections, it is somewhat hard to cure, however, a veterinarian can prescribe medicine that will heal most cases within two or three weeks. If the hooves have been neglected, the frog might be completely eaten away by the fungus; making the infection harder to cure. Thrush is one reason you should have a horse thoroughly examined by a veterinarian before you buy him. Signs of thrush are lameness, deterioration of the frog, and a strong, rotten odor.

Irregularities in the hoof wall. Cuts and blows to the coronet area may cause permanent damage to the cells which secrete the hoof wall. You may see long grooves growing down the hoof. Unless these grooves are deep enough to make the horse lame, they are not serious. Sometimes an injury to the coronet will cause all wall production in a small area to cease for a few days. This leaves a small hole in the hoof wall. The hole will finally grow out, and will probably cause no problems.

VICES

Vices in horses, like vices in people, are undesirable, compulsive habits. Vices are as hard to cure in horses as they are in people. You should avoid these habits like the plague:

Weaving. The animal will stand and sway from side to side. He will continually cross his feet over from one side to the other, and swing his head in wide arcs. Besides driving you crazy, this habit will make the horse hard to keep fat (he burns up a lot of energy weaving); it can cause founder in his front feet (he continues to weave with them long after they become sore from the activity); and it will spread to other horses in the stable (monkey see, monkey do). The original cause of weaving is probably boredom and restlessness from standing too long in a stall.

Cribbing. The horse will grab some hard object, such as a board on the fence, and swallow air with a belching sound. (Cribbing is not the same thing as eating wood, although these two habits are often confused.) Again, this vice will drive you crazy; cause your horse to be in poor condition, since he swallows air instead of food; and will spread to other horses. Also, horses which crib are likely to get colic from the air in their digestive tract. The causes are boredom and restlessness, and watching other horses that crib. People sometimes put cribbing collars (devices that fit around the throatlatch) on offending horses. Collars may or may not correct the problem: They will not cure it. If a horse is placed in a stall where he can find nothing to grab, he will not crib. However, he may start to wind suck instead.

Wind sucking. Wind sucking is "cribbing without hanging on." The horse will swallow air and belch, making terrible sounds, and ruining his digestive tract. Like cribbing, wind sucking is very contagious. The only possible correction is a cribbing collar. There is no cure.

Halter-pulling. A horse with this vice will refuse to stand tied. He may stand quietly for minutes, and then pull violently backwards, destroying his halter, the tie rope, the hitching rail, the barn wall, or whatever gives way first. This vice is caused by improper handling when the horse is very young. Sometimes horses learn to pull by being tied (while they are babies) with halters that are easily broken. The really bad halter pullers usually have been tied and whipped. They think it might happen again. Once the horse is confirmed in this habit, there is no real cure.

Biting. Any horse might nip or bite sometimes. Horses naturally nip each other in the pasture, and they will try the same trick on you if you let them. This type of biting is not a vice. The horse nips without malice: he is not trying to hurt you. Usually he will not hurt you, but will merely pinch your skin a little. A horse with the vice of biting is quite different: he is trying his best to sink his teeth into you. He wants to hurt you and he will be very sneaky about it. He will bite when you least expect it, and he will put all his strength into it. I've had horses bite through five layers of clothing and leave black bruises on my skin.

Prevention consists of always tying the animal when you work around him—and of always watching his head! Once you've been bitten, yelling at him and slapping him a few times on the neck might make an impression, but I wouldn't count on it.

Kicking. Some horses are more likely to kick than others. Under the proper circumstances, all horses will kick. If kicking is a vice, however, the horse will watch to catch you off your guard, and then let you have it. Yelling at the horse and letting him know you are not pleased—if you do this immediately—may keep this from happening again. You should always be wary of an animal that has been known to kick.

The vicious horse. Every now and then you run across a horse which is truly vicious. The viciousness may be overt or covert. An overtly vicious horse is easy to spot. He is usually a stallion, and he will be chained and muzzled. He makes it quite clear that he will tear you limb from limb if he gets a chance. The covertly vicious horse is more clever. He behaves like a gentleman while he watches for an opening. When he sees his chance, he is capable of anything. Fortunately, few vicious horses exist.

The frightened horse. The frightened horse is also capable of anything; however, his motivations are different from those of the vicious horse. The vicious horse is not frightened. The frightened horse may be so terrified that he breaks into a sweat. He shows his fear clearly by rolling his eyes, and by recoiling from your touch. He has either been abused or neglected. In both cases, he is a difficult horse to handle and cure. The prognosis is much better in the case of neglect, and it is best of all in the very young horse. The easiest and wisest thing, rather than buying a horse that shows fear, is to look for another horse.

HEALTH AND SOUNDNESS

Your veterinarian is the best judge of the health and soundness of your horse. You want to buy a horse free from disease and lameness. In general, you should look for a horse that is fat, with a smooth hair coat (a rough coat indicates worms). The animal should have no heavy or colored discharge from his nose or eyes, and no irregular bumps or swelling on his poll, withers, or legs. He should walk and trot smoothly, without stiffness, on both hard ground and soft. Both eyes should be clear, without spots or discolorations. His tongue should be free from grooves and splits caused by severe bits and rough hands.

Some diseases to watch for are as follows:

Swamp fever or equine infectious anemia (EIA). In the acute form, the disease will kill the horse. In the chronic form, it will render him thin and dull-looking. A fat, healthy horse may, however, be a carrier. Have the horse blood-tested by the vet before you buy.

Heaves. This is emphysema in the horse. He will have trouble breathing, and will cough up mucus through his nose.

Roaring. A horse that roars makes a loud sound when he breathes. This condition is caused by a thickening in the wind pipe, and might not show up unless the horse is galloped. Unless the roaring is very bad, you may be able to take lessons on the horse. However, he will never be completely sound, nor will he have the endurance of a sound horse.

Blindness. The horse should have good vision in both eyes. It is a good idea to have the animal's eyes checked carefully by a veterinarian. Partial or complete blindness is not uncommon, particularly in older horses.

Founder. (See "Feet" Chapter 1, page 19)

Lice or mange. (See "Tail" Chapter 1, page 5)

Body fungus. This shows up as grey, hairless patches on the skin. Horses also get ringworm, which will appear as round, red areas. Fungus can be cured, but it is highly contagious to other horses. The ringworm is also contagious to people.

Shipping fever. The horse will be feverish and dull. He will have a thick discharge from his nose. This disease is very contagious to other horses and can be serious.

Any open, running sores.

Worms and bots. In general, a horse must be wormed every six to eight weeks in order to be completely free of internal parasites. If the horse is thin, with a dull hair coat, he probably has worms. A fat horse is probably not heavily infested, but should be wormed after you buy him. Bots are flies which lay their eggs on the horse. Later the eggs hatch and the grubs enter the horse's mouth and grow in his stomach. Bot eggs are small, bright yellow dots that are glued to the hairs on the horse's legs and mane.

The veterinarian will check for major soundness problems; but he may not mention minor problems like a little fungus or a small sore. You should be there when the horse is examined so that he can answer all your questions. Be sure to ask the following questions:

1. How old is this horse?

2. Is his eyesight normal?

3. Does he have any fungus, mange, sores, or other skin conditions?

4. How is his breathing? Are his lungs and windpipe healthy?

5. Does he show any signs of illness?

6. If it is a mare, is she pregnant?

7. If it is a male horse, is he a stallion or a gelding? Sometimes horses are improperly gelded. They look like geldings but behave like stallions. Be sure to ask the veterinarian to check for this.

8. Are his feet healthy? Does the veterinarian think you will have any trouble with his feet in the future?

9. Does the horse have any problems that are making him lame now, or will make him lame in the future?

10. Does he need worming?

11. Is his general health good? Is he too fat or too thin?

12. Unless you have complete health records, ask the veterinarian to give the horse shots before you take it home. Horses should be inoculated against equine encephalomyelitis and tetanus every year in the spring.

A SUMMARY OF HORSE PSYCHOLOGY

In order to work with horses effectively, you must understand them. The more you keep in mind the following equine traits and characteristics, the greater will be your success.

HORSES ARE LARGE, SIMPLE ANIMALS

Never forget that horses are big. Big things are naturally clumsier and more destructive than small things. Horses are also rather stupid. They are not nearly as smart as a cat or dog. I have never seen evidence that a horse can learn by any method other than simple repetition.

HORSES ARE HERD ANIMALS

In nature, horses band together in herds for company and protection. Your horse will want to be with other horses. He will also copy the actions of other horses. If he sees a horse run, he will want to run. If he sees a horse crib, he will probably learn to crib.

IN NATURE, HORSES ARE PREY

They are hunted and eaten by predators. Humans are predators. As prey, horses are naturally nervous about strange movements and unfamiliar objects. They never know what is going to decide to eat them. It makes no difference that your horse has never been hunted. He still reacts like a hunted animal. Humans are hunters. You may never fire a gun, but your ancestors probably killed and ate horses. Therefore, your horse has an inborn fear of humans. You can train most of this fear out of him. However, if you frighten your horse, he will fight you as if he fears for his life.

HORSES DO NOT SEE AS WELL AS PEOPLE SEE

Horses have eyes that differ from humans' eyes to a great extent. We have eyes in the front of our heads, so that we see everything in three dimensions (length, height, width). Horses' eyes are on the sides of their heads, and they see most things from one eye at a time. Sometimes horses will see an object with one eye, and not know it is there with the other eye. This is why you should always speak as you move around your horse. You might frighten him when you walk into the range of the unseeing, unknowing eye. Nature designed horses' eyes to detect such dangers as mountain lions stalking in the grass. They see

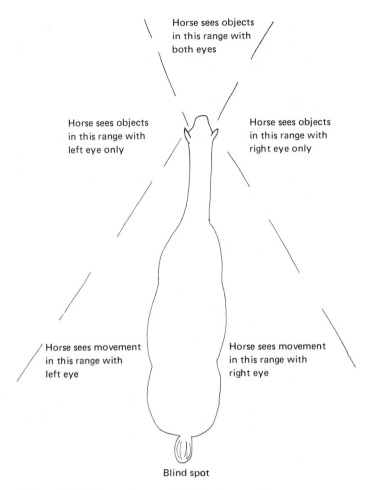

Figure 1–7. How a horse sees.

movement instantly, and frequently react before they think. Frequently your horse will be frightened by movement you don't see. When frightened, the horse's motto is "Run now; ask questions later."

HORSES ARE CREATURES OF HABIT

Horses learn through repetition. You should never allow your horse to repeat an undesirable act, such as kicking or running away. It is actually more important to prevent repetition than it is to punish, although wise punishment will help prevent the repetition of the act. Also, horses are more comfortable if everything about their life is kept at a routine. They prefer to eat, sleep, graze, and work at the same hours every day. Your horse will be happier and healthier if you establish a regular schedule.

HORSES CANNOT REASON

If your horse kicks you, and you wait ten minutes to punish him, he will not understand. He cannot connect the kicking with the punishment. You must always punish immediately after the infraction, and your punishment must be well placed and fair. If your horse kicks, a slap on the leg will do more good than a slap on the neck. Whipping him severely will merely make him nervous or resentful.

HORSES ARE ACCUSTOMED TO PECK ORDERS

In the herd, each horse has certain other horses it can kick, and certain other horses that can kick it. This peck order is not stable, but can change at any time. You tend to look upon your horse as a four-legged human; he looks upon you as a two-legged horse. He will try to place you in his peck order. It's to your interest to establish that you can kick him, but that he cannot kick you. If your horse acts aggressively towards you, by kicking or biting, slap him and yell "No!" When you do this, you are acting like a horse higher in the peck order than your horse: Such a horse would also kick and shout. The shout is as important as the kick. Horses rarely injure each other in these little battles: You need not really hurt your animal. A loud slap, accompanied with a shout, will do more good than a quiet beating. By the way, horses always hit each other on the body, and not on the legs or face. You should never hit your horse on the lower legs or the head. If he bites you, pop him in the chest—that's where another horse would let him have it.

HORSES DO HAVE EMOTIONS

Emotions come from the most primitive portions of the brain, and are common to all mammals. Thus, horses can feel bored, lonely, frightened, affectionate, angry, resentful, and sad. However, they rarely develop any true affection for humans. People should be regarded as masters rather than as close friends. A well-treated horse will respect his owner; and will show him trust and obedience.

In this chapter I discussed good and bad characteristics of horses, as well as certain traits all horses share. Hopefully, you will have a lot of help in selecting your mount. A friend will tell you if the animal is gentle, well-mannered and well-trained. A farrier will examine his feet and point out potential problems. A veterinarian will check the horse's health and soundness. If you take your time looking, and follow the advice of your helpers, you will probably obtain an ideal mount for your lessons in riding.

However, I don't suggest that you sit back and let others do all the work for you. You should study this chapter, and learn how horses are put together, and how they behave. Knowing how to ride a horse is more complex than knowing how to ride a bicycle. A bicycle will always turn if you turn the handlebars, and stop if you push on the brakes. Unfortunately, a horse is not so consistent in its behavior. A horse may stop if you pull on the reins, or he may pull on the bit and keep on going. It all depends on his previous training, his mood, and on such external factors as the time of day, and whether he is walking towards or away from the barn.

The point is that horses are living creatures. Unlike machines, they have minds and desires of their own. To ride well, you must not only learn to stay in the saddle, but also learn how your horse thinks. If you understand your horse you will be able to control him, and to win his trust and cooperation. Then you will experience the true joy of riding and horsemanship.

2 Equipment, Clothing, and Facilities

THE SADDLE AND BRIDLE

Three forms of riding are popular in this country today. These forms are western, or stock seat, huntseat (also called forward seat) and saddleseat riding. Huntseat and saddleseat are both called "English riding." In this book they will be discussed together under this term.

Figure 2-1 shows the parts of the stock saddle and the jumping saddle. Western saddles (stock saddles) come in many different sizes and styles. The best style for lessons is either the equitation saddle or the pleasure saddle. In order to tell whether the saddle fits you, straddle it, pressing your buttocks gently against the cantle (back) of the saddle. You should be able to lay a hand sideways between your thigh and the swells (front) of the saddle. If the seat feels too wide, look for a narrower model.

You should also straddle an English saddle for fit. Settle your weight into the lowest point of the seat, which should be in the middle of the saddle. Then lay a hand sideways in front of your crotch. You should have one hand's width to the front of the pommel. Behind, you should have one hand's width from your buttocks to the top of the cantle. Your knees should fit into the knee rolls when your legs are held in a comfortable position. Again, like Western saddles, English saddles come in different widths. If the saddle feels too wide, look for a narrower model.

29

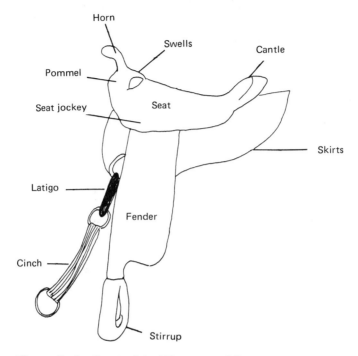

Figure 2–1. Parts of the Western saddle.

Western bits include hackamores, grazing bits, cutting bits, colt bits, and others. (See Figure 2-7.) Some people ride with a bosal. In these lessons, I recommend a mild bit such as a grazing bit. The first lessons should be ridden with an English snaffle, if one is available.

Bits commonly used in English riding include pelhams (used with the two sets of reins), kimberwickes, snaffles, dee rings (a form of snaffle), walking horse bits, and bradoon and curb (usually used together in a full bridle). (See Figures 2-4 to 2-6.) You should ride with a mild bit that allows you to use only a single set of reins. When the use of double reins is introduced, you may switch if you desire. There is no rule requiring the use of double reins in huntseat riding.

The snaffle is considered the mildest bit. Thick, light snaffles are milder than heavy or thin snaffles. In general, you should always ride with the mildest bit which gives you control

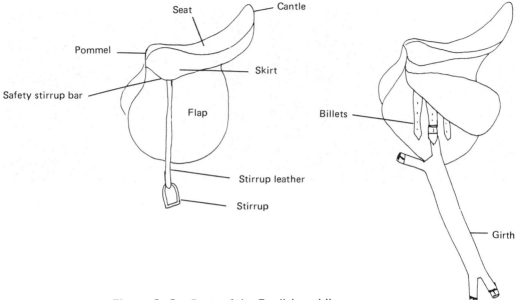

Figure 2–2. Parts of the English saddle.

of your horse. Twisted snaffles are very damaging to the horse's mouth, and should never be used.

    Kimberwickes are good bits for horses which are usually ridden in a pelham, a curb, or a Western bit, or for animals which—though basically gentle—will not allow a beginner to

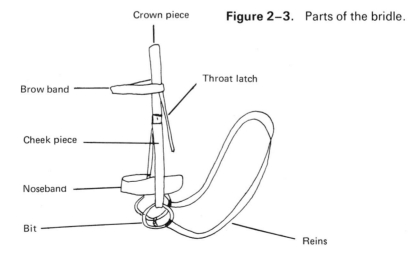

Figure 2–3. Parts of the bridle.

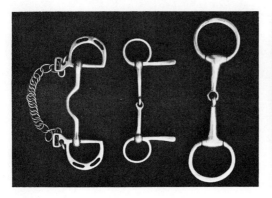 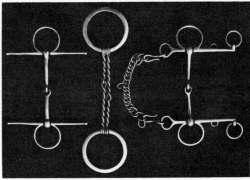

Figure 2–4. Whitmore kimberwicke (left), half-cheek snaffle or driving bit (center), egg-butt snaffle (right).

Figure 2–5. Full-cheek snaffle (left), double-twisted wire snaffle (center), jointed mouth pelham (right).

Figure 2–6. English bits.

Curb pelham

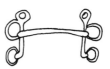

Mullen mouth pelham

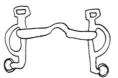

Whitmore kimberwicke

Eggbutt snaffle

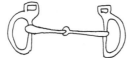

Jointed kimberwicke

Rubber snaffle

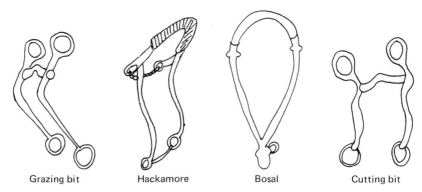

Grazing bit   Hackamore   Bosal   Cutting bit

Figure 2–7. Types of western bits.

control them with a snaffle. These bits have a curb chain, which should always be used. Kimberwickes are not particularly harsh bits, but they are too severe for tender-mouthed horses.

Pelhams are used to give greater control, usually on a horse which pulls and is slow in responding to a snaffle. Pelhams range from very mild to very severe.

Bradoons and curbs are used on saddleseat show horses to give them style. These bits are also sometimes used on huntseat horses for added control. With some exceptions, this is the most severe way to bit a horse. The horse must be trained to respond correctly to the double bits. This training is very complex, and must be performed by a skilled and experienced horseman. If the horse is not trained, a full bridle can cause both horse and rider much grief. Therefore, you should never put a full bridle on a horse that has not received special schooling.

Western riders use not only different saddles than English riders, but also different bits. The Western-tacked horse is bitted with a Western curb bit. This bit differs in shape from the English curb bit. However, all curb bits are generally considered severe bits. A curb is a bit with a port, and a chain or strap under the chin. This type of bit acts as a lever on the horse's jaw. The lever action magnifies any pressure you put on the reins. Thus a light touch on the reins—a slight pull—will be a strong pull on the horse's jaw.

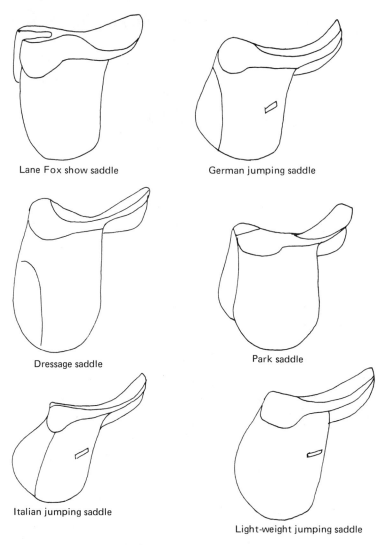

Lane Fox show saddle

German jumping saddle

Dressage saddle

Park saddle

Italian jumping saddle

Light-weight jumping saddle

Figure 2–8. Types of English saddles.

OTHER EQUIPMENT

Types of Halters

Halter is the term used in this country for the rope or leather headpiece used in leading and tying a horse. Novices frequently confuse the words "halter" and "bridle." In order to keep these

34

straight, remember that a bridle has a bit, and is used in riding the horse; and that a halter doesn't have a bit, and is used as a collar is used on a dog—for leading and tying only.

Several different types of halters are available. All types come in different sizes to fit all size horses. The three major halter types are those made from leather, nylon, and rope. Leather halters look the nicest, and do not rub the hair off the horse's face. They are also hard for the horse to lose in the pasture. However, leather halters are the most expensive, and the most easily broken. Nylon halters are very sturdy; they don't break or pull off. However, they will rub the hair off, disfiguring the horse's face, in some cases. Rope halters, also very sturdy, are made of cotton rope or polypropylene. They are the least expensive, but also the least attractive halters. They come off easily when the horse rubs his ears on his legs, or on the fence.

Lead Straps and Tie Ropes

Lead straps are made of leather or nylon. On one end is a brass or brass-coated chain and snap. Of the two, the leather lead strap with the brass chain is the best. Leather will not give you burns on your hands if the horse should pull away, and solid brass will not wear away or tarnish. Since the chain on the lead strap is designed for extra control, like the choke chain of a dog collar, it is not necessary with many gentle horses. Usually, you can lead your horse with the tie rope. Incidently, unless you wish to risk breakage, you should never tie your horse with the lead strap.

Tie ropes are fiber or nylon ropes with a snap braided into one end. They are used to tie the horse, and, in many cases, to lead him. The snap is attached to the halter, and the loose rope is held in your hands. You can easily make your own tie rope. Buy six to ten feet of rope and a good, sturdy snap. The rope may be of any kind: Nylon will not absorb water, but cotton is the softest. A round-eye swivel snap about three and one quarter inches long makes the most convenient snap. You can braid the rope through the eye of the snap. It doesn't matter how neat the braiding looks. The loose end of the rope should be knotted or braided to prevent unraveling.

Grooming Equipment

You will need more grooming equipment if you buy your own horse than if you borrow or rent a horse. Usually, if the horse belongs to others, the owners will supply you with the necessary brushes and other grooming items. Grooming for riding is discussed in another paragraph (see Chapter 3). For a complete grooming you will need a dandy brush (stiff bristles), a body brush (soft bristles), a mane comb, a hoof pick, a rubber curry comb, a towel, and a sweat scraper. Other useful items are fly repellent, hoof dressing, and a mild wound dressing such as vaseline or nitrofurazone dressing.

Boots and Bandages

Sometimes we find it necessary to put special forms of protection on our horses' legs. You will not need to worry about this with most horses during the more elementary lessons; however, it is a good idea to be familiar with boots and bandages.

Boots are used on horses that hit themselves when they move, and on horses which might injure themselves on some object during their work. Of course, it is not desirable for a horse to be knocking his legs together, but many of them do. Most commonly, horses will cut their forelegs with the hooves of their back legs. Bell boots—rubber bell-shaped devices—protect the coronet and hoof from blows. Polo boots and galloping boots protect the cannon bones. Ankle boots are made for fetlocks, while knee or hock boots cover the knees or hocks. Run-down boots protect the sesamoid bones at the back of the fetlock. Shipping boots are made for all four legs and are used to protect the legs from bruising during transport.

Bandages also protect the legs during exercise. They are

used in the stable to prevent swelling of the legs after work, and to hold dressings in place. Bandages come in several different types: cotton stable or track bandages, with ties or velcro tapes; elastic bandages; latex bandages; nylon bandages; and foam reinforced bandages. Bandages should always be applied over padding (quilted cotton cloth or sheet cotton) and wrapped snuggly, but not tightly enough to cut off circulation.

Sheets, Blankets, and Coolers

Stable sheets are lightweight, fitted covers for the horse. Stable blankets are also fitted, and padded to provide the horse with protection from the cold. Actually, most horses don't seem to mind cold weather. If horses are sheltered from the north wind and from dampness, they can usually go all winter with only their own coats for protection. I use blankets for old or sick horses, and for horses that are being stressed in some way, such as being trailered to a show.

Blanketing a horse will not—contrary to popular belief—keep him from growing a winter coat of hair. Some horses grow much more winter hair than others. They inherit their coats from their ancestors, and they grow them each year in response to the shortening lengths of the days.

Blankets make the hair lie down and look prettier. They do not keep it from growing. Many people don't like their horses to get fuzzy in the fall. They clip off the hair with electric clippers. If you do this, then you must protect your horse by replacing his hair with a good warm blanket. It's a good idea to buy machine washable blankets, although they cost more. A horse can get a blanket very dirty.

Coolers are large covers used to help a horse cool out after exercise. If you are careful not to bring your mount back to the stable lathered with sweat, you won't need one. It's a good idea to always cool your horse before you take him to the barn. (See Chapter 3 for more information.) You can ride him quietly at a walk until he stops sweating. By doing this you cool your horse slowly, and help avoid equine colds and other illnesses.

Special Equipment

Two special types of equipment might be of use to you in controlling your mount. These are martingales and dropped nosebands.

MARTINGALES

Several different types of martingales exist, and each has a different specific use and value. Many horsepeople believe that a well-trained horse should never need a martingale. Others believe that martingales are valuable aids in training and riding. In these beginning lessons, we will use martingales only when necessary, and only for their most basic purpose: to keep the horse from holding its head too high, thus making it harder for you to control him. Note that martingales never keep a horse from tossing his head up and down, as many people believe.

The running martingale attaches by loose rings to the snaffle reins. (see Figure 2-9). It can be used with any bridle, and sometimes it is used to help control the horse on the turns while jumping, as well as to keep the horse from throwing his head up too high. Running martingales frequently interfere with the action of the reins. You should not use one except, perhaps, in jumping.

Standing martingales—sometimes called tie-downs—attach to a regular noseband on the bridle (see Figure 2-9). Their only action is to keep the horse from raising his head above the proper level. If you must use a martingale, use this kind.

Other types of martingales are the Irish martingale and the German martingale. These types are less popular than the kinds mentioned above.

The Irish martingale is a short strap that has a ring on each end. This strap is placed on the reins—one rein through each ring—and allowed to slide up and down under the horse's neck. It keeps the reins together. I think you will have better success

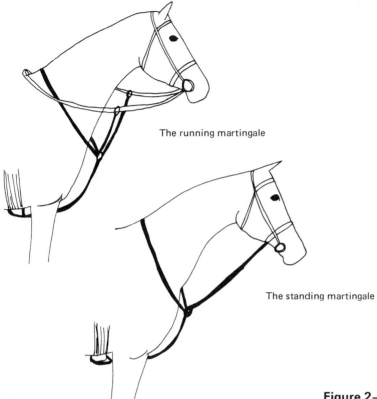

The running martingale

The standing martingale

Figure 2–9. Martingales.

in these lessons if your reins are loose, so you can easily use one rein at a time.

The German martingale was designed for use by Olympic riders on jumping courses. It is a very severe type of running martingale. You certainly will not need such a severe device if you are riding a well-trained horse. You will be happiest, and your horse will be most content, if you use as few devices as possible.

DROPPED NOSEBANDS

Dropped nosebands are used on a huntseat snaffle bridle to keep the horse from opening his mouth too wide. If a horse throws his mouth open, a snaffle bit has little effect. These nosebands are used in place of a regular noseband, and should be used only with snaffle bits. They make other types of bits too severe, as a horse wearing a dropped noseband cannot yield properly to a pelham or curb. Dropped nosebands may be adjusted above or below the bit, depending upon the length of the horse's mouth. A horse with a long mouth would take the noseband below the bit. On a short-mouthed animal, there is no room below the bit for the noseband, and it must be put on above the bit. Dropped nosebands should be tightened only to the point where you can get three fingers flat between the top of the horse's muzzle and the noseband. If the noseband is pulled too tight, it will keep the horse from opening his mouth slightly to yield with his jaw. This will interfere with the development of "feel" (or the ability to communicate with your horse through the reins) in your hands in later lessons.

RIDING CLOTHES

Frequently, beginners don't ride in suitable clothes. They try to cut costs by riding in whatever they happen to have in their closets, without realizing that comfortable riding clothes are as important to their progress in learning to ride as is a saddle and a good horse. Suitable clothes protect you from bruises, blisters, sunburn, and concussion. I suggest that you buy or borrow at least one outfit—it can be the most inexpensive available. Later on, as you get more experience in riding, you will be better able to decide what types and styles of dress you prefer.

Western Wear

For learning Western riding, you will need jeans, or other heavy duty, snug pants. Don't get jeans that are too tight; they will keep you from moving freely in the saddle. Any comfortable shirt will do. Boots are essential: Western boots are best. Women may be able to buy inexpensive boots from the boys' shoe department. Many stores sell serviceable boots for boys casual wear. Good Western-style boots are always available at Western clothing stores. You need a boot with a high top, a pointed or tapered toe, and a heel that will not accidentally slip through the stirrup. Many Western boots have a built-up heel designed to catch on the stirrup and keep the foot in place. If you ride in shoes or boots without a built-up heel, your foot might go through and become caught. I've had this happen more than once. It can be very distressing to try to get your foot unstuck if the horse is standing quietly; and if the horse decides to move off, a stuck foot can be fatal. Hats protect your face, and eyes, from the sun. Gloves will keep your hands from becoming calloused and blistered.

Huntseat and Saddleseat Clothing

Comfortable riding outfits for saddleseat lessons include jodhpurs, jodhpur boots or heavy shoes, a comfortable shirt, a hat, and gloves. For huntseat riding, you may dress as above, or you may wear breeches and hunt boots, or jeans and hunt boots, or casual pants and polo chaps with jodhpur boots or hunt boots (see Figure 2-10). It is important in English riding to protect your knees. They undergo a lot of wear against the saddle. Therefore, you should not try to ride in jeans—unless you wear tall hunt boots. Western boots are usually too stiff to allow for the movements in the foot and ankle that are necessary in English-style riding.

For jumping, you must have some sort of hard hat. Those made for riding are the most suitable. Hunt caps will do, if you wear the chin strap. However, they tend to be rather hot in the summer. Schooling helmets, made of caliente or fiberglas, and ventilated with a few holes, are both lighter and cooler. These caps should have a safety harness, and an inner cushion and air space.

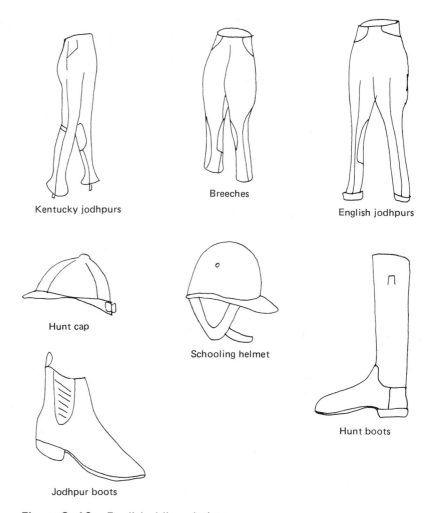

Kentucky jodhpurs

Breeches

English jodhpurs

Hunt cap

Schooling helmet

Hunt boots

Jodhpur boots

Figure 2–10. English riding clothes.

What Not to Wear

Do not ride in sneakers, sandals, loafers, or other light or loose shoes. Such shoes are dangerous. Your foot may slip through the stirrup and become hung. Also, these shoes allow your ankle to bang against the hard stirrup, producing blisters and sores. Loafers will slide off your heel when you take the correct leg position.

Here is a group of further "don'ts" important to remember. Don't wear shorts, unless you also wear chaps. You will blister your knees, and you will be unable to maintain the correct leg position. Don't wear tight clothing. You should be able to freely move each joint. Don't wear long, floating scarves or other loose, flapping clothing. It may frighten your mount, or become hung up on the ring. Don't try to ride holding an umbrella. Don't jump, even a little, without a hard hat.

RIDING FACILITIES

The Riding Ring

In order to follow the lessons in this book, you must have some sort of riding ring (see Figure 2-11). Perhaps there is a ring available for your use. If not, you may have to build one. The ring should be rectangular, though you can learn in an oval, round, or square ring if necessary. It is important that the ring be safe—it should contain no trees, bushes, or other obstacles. For the first lessons, there should be no jumps or other training aids in the riding ring. The ground of the riding area should be fairly soft—but it should not be deep sand—and should have no rocks or garbage scattered around. The ring must be fenced! A suitable fence is one three and one half to four feet high, made of one or more boards or rails, with a gate that closes and hooks. No wire should be used in the ring fence. Wire is dangerous. It is too easy to catch your foot or to get cut. The height of the fence is also important. A fence that is too low will encourage the horses to step or leap over. A too high fence leads to small horses ducking under the top railing. Needless to say, if there is a rail at four feet or so, other rails may be higher without affecting the safety of the fence. As for the gate, if it does not close and hook, the horses will quickly learn to push it open and leave the ring. As a beginner rider, you may find such tricks hard to pre-

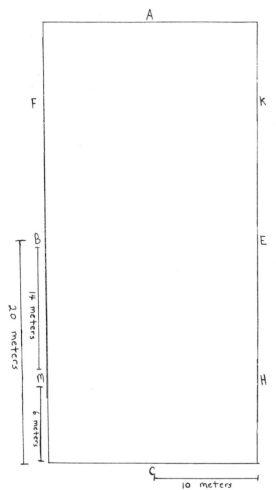

Figure 2–11. The riding ring should be twice as long as it is wide. The gate should be midway on one of the short ends. The ends should be square. Letters should be placed as follows:

A   In the gate
C   Midway down the opposite side of the ring
B,E   Midway down the long sides of the ring
F,K   15% of the distance of the long sides, starting from A
M,H 15% of the distance of the long sides, starting from C

If your ring measures 20 meters by 40 meters, the letters will be placed as shown in the diagram.

vent; and it is better not to take chances than to get a fast, free ride to the stable.

You will need the following letters on your riding ring: A,C,H,E,K,M,B,F. These letters will help you understand the exercises I will discuss in the lessons. For example, I may tell you to trot from M to K. If you do not have letters in your ring, you will not have the slightest idea of where you should go. They should be painted on plywood, and be large enough to be clearly visible. On your own ring, you may nail them to the fence posts. If the ring is not yours, you may hang the letters with cord, and remove them when you finish riding. Figure 2-11 indicates the proper spacing for the letters.

Cavaletti

Cavaletti are a series of low rails, arranged in a row. Cavaletti have many uses. We are going to use simple cavalletti exercises as an aid to developing your riding skills. Usually, these exercises are associated with jumping. However, they are just as useful in Western and saddleseat riding as a training tool. Cavaletti teach the horse to pick up his feet, and to cross strange obstacles. They also help teach the rider control.

You will need seven cavaletti. Figure 2-12 shows you a simple way to make them.

Figure 2–12. Cavaletti.

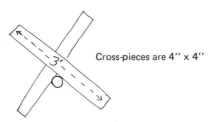

Cross-pieces are 4″ x 4″

Rail is attached off-center so that rolling the cavaletti varies its height.

Rail is 9′ or 10′ long. It should be a rounded 4″ x 4″ and bolted in place.

Jumps

You need not borrow or make jumps if you are learning Western or saddleseat riding, or if you do not wish to learn to jump. If you are learning huntseat and wish to jump, you need at least three complete jumps. The post and rail type are best for these lessons. The jumps need not be tall—three or four feet is enough—but they must be sturdy and safe. Treated lumber will last longer. Do not make jumps less than twelve feet wide. Narrow jumps are too easy for the horse to avoid. You should buy jump cups. Jump cups are metal or plastic devices, which are

Figure 2–13.   Jumps.

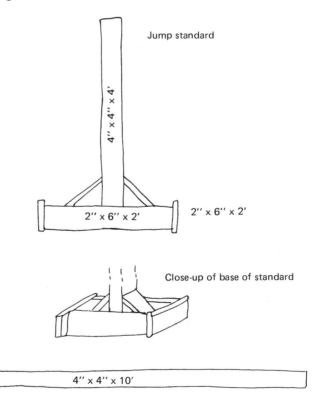

Jump standard

4″ x 4″ x 4′

2″ x 6″ x 2′   2″ x 6″ x 2′

Close-up of base of standard

4″ x 4″ x 10′

Use a rounded 4″ x 4″ at least 10′ long for the jump rail.
Attach it to the standards with jump cups.

attached to the jump standards, and hold the jump rail. Some people try to support the rails with nails or wooden spikes; but this is rarely satisfactory, and may be dangerous. Cups allow the rail to release and fall if your horse (or you) should make a mistake and hit the jump. If the rail did not fall, it could splinter and be transformed into a deadly lance. The rails should be at least four inches in diameter (bamboo fishing poles are not suitable) and should be painted in bright colors in order to improve visibility. Figure 2–13 shows an easy way to make safe jumps.

Bending Poles

You will need bending poles of some sort so you can follow the exercises in the lessons. If you make jumps, you may use jump standards wherever bending poles are required. Otherwise, you should come up with some sort of safe marker that you can easily move in and out of the ring. You may simply stick bamboo rods into the dirt, or turn a few large plastic buckets upside down. The important thing is to have some sort of marker that you can both ride around and move around. You will need, in later exercises, to ride patterns around these markers (or bending poles). You will also need to be able to change the positions of the poles or markers for different exercises.

Now that you have read about the clothing, and equipment you will need to learn to ride, you might be having a few second thoughts about the matter. Perhaps you think that all this attention to other things isn't necessary—all you need to ride is a horse! Or, perhaps you are thinking that riding is too complex, and not really worth all this trouble. Actually, neither thought is exactly true.

You can learn to ride with only a horse and a bridle, but you will probably not learn very well. A certain amount of special equipment is necessary. After all, you wouldn't try to learn tennis without a ball and racket—and you wouldn't try to learn to swim without a bathing suit! The clothing and equipment I mention in this chapter will protect you while you ride, enable you to learn to ride as quickly as possible, and help your lessons go smoothly.

Riding is very complex. It is probably one of the most complex sports of all. To learn to ride well takes book knowledge, hours of practice, careful attention to detail, and special clothing and equipment. However, I think you will find that riding is not too complex to be mastered. If you really like horses, and really want to be with them and to have fun on horseback, you can find ways to obtain all the clothing and equipment that you need.

Remember that these lessons are designed for you to give to yourself! You are your own teacher; you won't have a trained instructor. Therefore, you will need to provide your own teaching-aids (the suggested equipment) if you wish to learn to ride quickly and well. The equipment I discuss in this chapter will make riding easier and more interesting for you during these lessons. If you follow this book closely, and provide yourself with the recommended clothing and equipment, you should find that you are a good teacher and a good pupil. You will find that you really can enjoy riding your horse!

TEST: PART I, CHAPTERS 1-2

Answers to these test questions and to the other tests in the book, may be found in the Appendix.

1. Write the following terms in the proper locations on the photograph of the horse shown in Figure 2–14:

Neck	Barrel	Point of rump
Croup	Forearm	Gaskin
Withers	Shoulder	Fetlock
Tail	Eye	Hoof
Stifle	Chin	Knee
Chestnut	Lips	Point of
Coronet	Poll	shoulder
Heart	Back	Throttle
Nostril	Crest	Jaw
Cannon	Hock	Loins
Pastern		Point of hip

Figure 2–14. Test picture: parts of the horse.

2. Describe briefly each of the following colors:

    a. Dun   e. Seal brown   i. Palomino

    b. Black   f. Appaloosa   j. Roan

    c. Chestnut   g. Buckskin   k. Grey

    d. Bay   h. Pinto   l. White

3. Write the following terms in the proper location on the diagram of the Western and English saddle (Figures 2–15a, b):

Cantle	Billets	Girth
Pommel	Cinch	Leathers
Horn	Stirrup	Stirrup Bar
Swells	Flap	Seat
Fender	Skirts	

4. Fill in the terms in the proper place on the English bridle (Figure 2–15c):

Noseband	Crown piece	Bit
Reins	Noseband	Cheek piece
Throat latch		

5. Discuss briefly the purpose of the martingale and of the dropped-noseband. Name the four types of martingales.

Figure 2–15. Test picture: saddles and bridle.

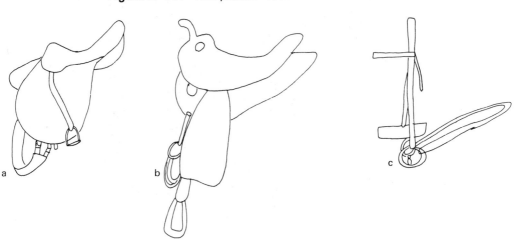

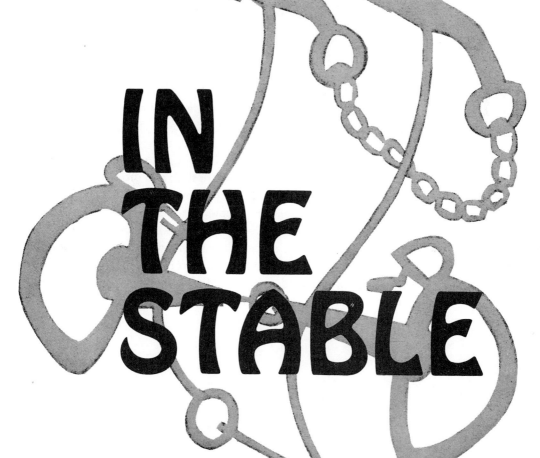

11

IN THE STABLE

Riding is far from the only aspect of horsemanship. Sooner or later you will either need, or want, to handle your horse in the stable. This part is designed with this in mind. Chapter 3 discusses catching and leading a horse—a necessary procedure, as horses do not come and heel like a dog. Chapter 4 goes over tying and grooming. In general, horses will not stand unless they are tied; and grooming is as important to the horse as your personal grooming is to you. Chapter 5 introduces you to problems in the stable. A novice can easily get into a lot of trouble in the stable due to ignorance of how the horse should behave. This chapter discusses frequently observed forms of bad behavior, with preventions and cures. Part II ends with tests. To check your learning progress, you should take the tests. You can find the correct answers in the text, or in the Appendix.

3 How to Catch, Lead, and Lunge Your Horse

IN THE STALL

Get the horse's attention before you enter the stall. Remember, horses frequently doze while standing with their eyes open. If you walk up too suddenly, you may startle him, and he may turn and kick. Nowadays, most horses are kept loose in a box stall. To catch a horse from a box stall, stand at the door and call to him. He will probably walk up to the door. Step inside, stand by his left shoulder, and put on the halter. Do not leave the door open while you put the halter on him. Many horses will rush out and bolt away from you if they have the chance.

If your horse is tied in a straight stall, or if he refuses to come to the door of a box stall, enter the stall carefully. Talk to him. Let him know where you are at all times. As you approach him, touch him gently while standing out of the way of his feet. You don't want to be hurt should he kick. Walk slowly to his head and attach the halter and lead strap.

Once you have left the stall, you should hook the stall door so that it will not swing or be in the way. Be careful as you lead your animal in and out of his stall. The door should be opened wide enough to allow the animal easy passage. If he thinks the door is closing on him, he will rush forward or pull back; and he may injure himself, or you.

53

IN THE PASTURE

Some horses will come to the pasture gate either when you call them, or at certain times each day. They are more likely to do this if you feed them when they are caught, or if they are pastured alone. If your horse is out with other horses, or if the pasture is large, you will probably need to walk out after him.

I suggest that you carry a halter and lead strap and walk slowly towards your horse. It's not a good idea to take a feed bucket if your horse is grazing with other horses. The other horses will crowd around you and fight over the feed. You may carry a carrot in your pocket, however. Approach your mount from the front. Horses are less likely to move away from you if you come towards them head-on. Start talking to him when you get a hundred feet or so away. You don't want to startle him, as he may turn and run from you. When you get within a few feet

Figure 3–1. To catch your horse in the pasture, approach him from the front. Then step to the side and run your hand down his neck. Your horse will probably behave as Anrock does and try to grab as much grass as possible before you take him to the barn. Notice that Anrock is too big for his rider; you should learn on a horse that is better suited to you in size.

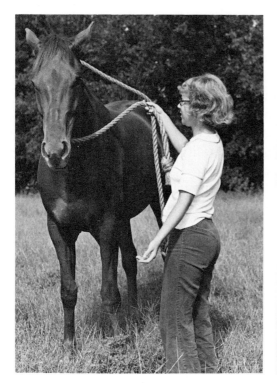 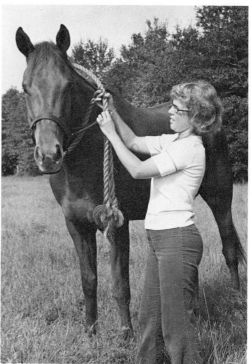

Figure 3-2 and 3-3. *Left* Put the rope around your horse's neck before you try to halter him. Some horses will turn and run away as soon as they see the halter. If you have the rope on the neck, you have control. You should not turn your horse out to graze wearing his halter as he may lose it or get hung up on something and hurt himself. *Right* You can buckle the halter in place without letting go of the lead rope. Don't wrap the lead rope around your arm or throw it over your shoulder; you might be hurt if your horse did something unexpected. Once the halter is buckled, you can snap the lead rope to its ring and take your mount to the barn.

of him, hold out your hand—or the carrot. Then run your hand down his neck, and draw the lead strap around his neck. Step back to his left side, and slip the halter on your horse. Move cautiously until you have the animal secured. Some horses are easier to catch if you persuade them with soft words. Others must be ordered to "Whoa!" in a firm voice. Some will sniff for the carrot, and run off if you neglected to bring it. If your horse should move away from you, walk after him. Try to circle until you are directly in front of him, and try again. Never run after the horse. This will merely tend to excite him, and make him harder to catch. Most horses will stop and let themselves be caught when they see that you are not going to leave without them. Horses will not run far from their equine friends. As long as your beast is the only one fleeing, you have an excellent chance of grabbing him sooner or later. A trick which works when all else fails is this: Catch another horse, preferably a close friend of your horse (horses usually have one or two bosom buddies). Then walk slowly towards your horse, keeping this animal between you. When you catch up to your horse, you will probably be able to slip the lead strap around his neck.

LEADING YOUR HORSE

Attach the lead strap or tie rope to the ring at the bottom of the halter. If you use a lead strap, you may also run the chain either under or over the nose for added control.

Standing on the left side of the horse—called his near side; the right side is the off side—place your right hand on the lead strap about six inches below the halter ring. Hold the loose end of the strap folded in your left hand. Do not wrap the strap around your hand. If your horse should be frightened, he might bolt and run off. You want to be able to let go of the strap if necessary. People have been dragged and injured because they couldn't let go. I know of a boy who lost three fingers when a calf bolted. The rope was around his hand, and it tightened, and pulled the fingers off his hand. Needless to say, you should never wrap the lead strap around your neck or waist.

When you are ready to move, give a little tug to get your horse's attention, and begin walking. Walk to the left of the horse. Do not walk directly in front of him. Remember our little discussion on how horses sometimes bolt? If he bolts and you are in front of him, he will run you down. If your animal doesn't follow immediately, give a stronger tug on the strap. If he abso-

Figure 3–4. When leading your horse, always walk on his left side, with his head by your right shoulder. You may snap the lead rope to the bottom ring of the halter or run the chain under your horse's chin, as in this picture. Be careful to walk far enough away from your horse to keep him from stepping on your heels!

lutely refuses to follow, you can give a sharp pull off to the left. This will throw the horse off balance, making him take a step. Once he starts walking, he will probably forget his stubbornness.

In order to stop a horse while you are leading it, give a tug backwards on the halter. If he is walking too fast, make him stop and stand for a moment. Then try again. There is little you can do by yourself for a horse that walks too slowly. Screaming and tugging don't usually do the trick. A friend walking behind the stubborn beast with a whip works wonders.

When you come to a gate, make your horse stop and stand. Unlatch the gate and open it away from you, just wide enough for you and the horse to get through. Don't fling it all the way open, especially if other horses are in the pasture. They might follow you out. As soon as your horse is out of the gate, turn him to face it. Close the gate, and redo the latch. It is possible, but more difficult, to get the horse through when the gate opens towards you. Then you must unlatch the gate, and persuade your beast to move around the open end to walk out. Then you usually must make him step backwards a pace or two so that you can draw the gate closed.

LUNGING

Lunging is a method of exercising and training a horse while you remain on the ground. You may lunge your horse on days when you cannot ride, in order to keep him in condition. If your mount has been standing in a stall for a while, lunging before you ride will calm him and make him easier for you to control.

Properly speaking, you should use a special device called a "lunging caveson." However, if you do not have access to this piece of equipment, you may lunge the horse you are learning on with a halter. Work in a lunging ring—a round ring 40 to 60 feet in diameter—or in a corner of the riding ring (see Figure 3-10). Lunging is easiest in a special, round ring (see Figure 3-9).

Follow these steps:

1. Saddle and bridle your horse. Either leave the halter on under the bridle, or place the lunging caveson (or halter) on over the bridle.

Figure 3–5. Anrock is wearing a lunging caveson. The caveson has heavy metal bands that fit around the nose for a great deal of control. The jaw straps should be tight, in order to keep the cheek pieces out of the horse's eyes. The lunge line snaps to the middle ring on the nose.

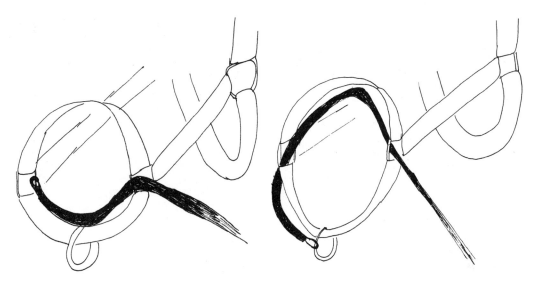

Figure 3–6a,b. Lunging with the halter: (a) the line should be drawn up under the nose and not simply attached to the ring of the halter: (b) drawing the line over the nose gives more control.

2. Hook the reins under the stirrups. You may unbuckle the reins and tie each rein to the billets.

3. Attach the lunge line—a web strap about 25 feet long—to the middle ring on the nose of the caveson. If you are using a halter, run the line under the nose of your mount.

4. Pick up the loose end of the line in your left hand (if you are lunging to the left). Hold the line so that it does not wrap around your hand.

5. Hold the lunge whip in your right hand (if lunging to the left). Keep the whip pointed at the horse at all times.

6. Drive the horse forward with the whip. Stay even with his shoulder. Keep a little slack in the lunge line, if possible.

7. Use voice commands—walk, trot, walk, halt. Never canter or gallop on the lunge.

8. If your horse refuses to move, pop the whip behind him. Slap the whip across his haunches if necessary.

9. If the animal moves into the circle, use the whip on his side to move him back to the fence.

10. If he refuses to slow, be patient. Apply steady pressure on the line and repeat "Easy, Walk," until he responds. Do not jerk the line, as

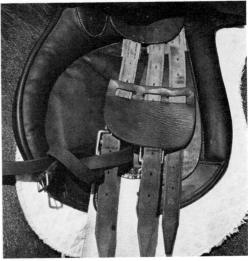

Figure 3–7. Here is an easy way to tie up the stirrup on an English saddle for lunging. Western stirrups can be removed or tied over the seat of the saddle with cord.

Figure 3–8. On an English saddle, you can unbuckle the reins and tie them loosely to the billets for lunging. Western reins may be tied loosely to the latigos.

Figure 3–9. Lunging in a lunging ring.

Figure 3–10. Lunging in a corner of the riding ring.

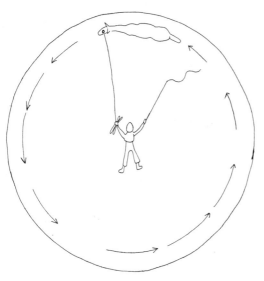

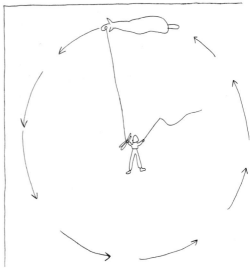

Figure 3–11. Hold the lunge line folded so that it does not wrap around your hand. If you fold it into figure-eight loops, you can gradually play out more line to your horse. Leather gloves will keep you from getting burns on your hands.

Figure 3–12. Chocolate is trotting nicely on the lunge. The lunge line is over her nose and attached to the other side of the halter for control. She is moving on the track of the lunging ring. The trainer holds the lunge line in her left hand. She has a whip in her right hand. Chocolate's martingale is tied up and not attached to the bridle while she exercises on the lunge.

Figure 3–13. Now Chocolate is galloping, something your horse should never do on the lunge. She is fighting her trainer, who wants her to slow to a trot. The halter does not give enough control for the animal that wants to misbehave. A lunging caveson would be much better in this case.

you will pull his head in sharply and you may cause him to strain his shoulder or neck. Also, sharp tugs on the line may pull the halter or caveson into his eye, causing damage. You may jingle the line a little, but do not jerk it.

11. Don't gallop on the lunge. Your horse might pull away from you, and he is sure to hurt his legs sooner or later. To keep control of your horse, and to avoid possible accidents, walk and trot him on the lunge only.

4 How to Tie and Groom Your Horse

HOW TO TIE YOUR HORSE

For the sake of safety, you should always tie your horse while you groom him, saddle him, or do other work around him. Tying keeps him from wandering, and helps prevent kicks and bites. Many people prefer cross-ties. If you have no cross-ties available, you must tie with a single rope. You should follow these safety rules:

1. Never tie by the lead strap. Your horse may pull back and pulverize it. Use the tie rope.

2. Never tie by the reins of the bridle, or by a rope snapped to the bit of the bridle. If the horse pulls back, he will tear the bridle, and perhaps his mouth, to shreds.

3. Tie to something solid. A horse weighs around 1,000 pounds. Don't tie him to anything that might pull up, or break, or drag. I see horses (all the time!) tied to boards in the fence or ring. This is destructive and dangerous. A little pull by the horse may break the board and jerk the loose end into his face or chest. Tie your horse to sturdy posts, trees, or specially made hitching rails ONLY! NEVER tie a horse to wire or board fences, the riding ring, car doors, lawn chairs, rubber tires, tree branches, stall guards, light-pole guide wires, jumps, or any other unstable or breakable object.

4. Don't give the horse too much slack, and don't tie the rope too low. The rope should be tied three or four feet from the ground with only two or three feet of slack. If the rope is too loose or too low, the

horse may catch a foot, and panic. Horses have broken legs and necks this way.

5. Don't tie your horse and leave him unattended. You should watch him, or at least check up on him every fifteen to twenty minutes.

6. Don't tie your horse with a long rope so he can graze. He will probably tie his legs together and get rope burns, if not a broken leg or neck. If you want to graze your horse in an open area, it is best to hold him on a lead rope.

I think horses must study with some present-day Houdini, because they are able to work even the most elaborate knots loose and get free. Or, if they don't get the knot loose, they tighten it to the point where you can't get it free either. Actually, there is a simple solution to this problem. It is a variation of the slip knot that I call the "horse knot." If you use this knot

Figure 4–1. The horse tying knot is easy to make. Simply tie a loop around the rope with the free end. Another name for this knot is the slip knot.

correctly, your horse will stay tied, and you will be able to get the rope loose later. To tie the "horse knot" follow these steps:

1. Place the free end of the rope around the post or rail that you are using to anchor your horse. Bring it back towards you.

2. Put the free end of the rope over the top of the rope that goes to your horse's head.

3. Bring the free end completely around the rope to make a loop.

4. Now, stick the free end of the rope through the loop. Tighten the loop slightly by pulling on the free end of the rope.

5. Double the free end of the rope and pull it back through the loop, making a second loop.

6. Stick the free end of the rope through the second loop and pull tight.

You now have your horse tied so that he cannot pull free, or untie himself. You can easily undo the knot by following these two steps:

1. Pull the free end of the rope out of the second loop.

2. Pull on the free end of the rope. The knot will come untied.

If this explanation confuses you, study the pictures in Fig-

Figure 4–2. You can make the knot easier to untie if you slip the free end of the rope back through the loop. A quick pull on the rope end will free your mount.

ures 4-1 and 4-2. Then, you might practice tying the knot until it becomes easy for you. This knot will make life a lot more pleasant for you. It is simple to tie, and will come loose even if your horse happens to pull back on the rope. Other knots will tighten under tension, and "freeze up." I've cut many a rope to free my horse in the past, before I started using the "horse knot."

GROOMING BEFORE YOU RIDE

I'm not going to discuss the daily, complete grooming your horse should have to keep him healthy and attractive. **The Manual of Horsemanship of the British Horse Society and Pony Club,** published by the British Horse Society, is filled with useful information and helpful hints on grooming. You can find directions in many other books telling you how to curry your horse, how to pull his mane, and when to use hoof dressings and wound ointments. Complete care is not in the scope of this book. However, no matter how well-groomed the horse is in general, you should always give him a brief cleaning before you saddle and bridle him. You do this quick grooming in order to remove dirt from under the saddle, and to check the condition of his feet.

First, tie your horse. Then, with a dandy brush, brush his back and sides in the direction of hair growth. You may brush his mane, tail, and legs, if you desire. Next, take a soft, clean towel, or a body brush, and brush his face and ears. If you find any untreated cuts or lumps, you should point them out to the horse's owner. Put a little wound dressing on the cuts if the horse is yours. Cuts under the girth or saddle may be caused by your tack. If you find saddle sores, give your horse a few days' rest, and use more padding under your saddle. With girth sores, you must rest your horse until they heal. Buy a softer girth, or one designed to be chafeless.

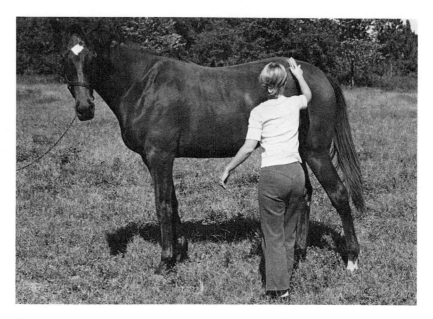

Figure 4–3. Most horses enjoy being brushed. Chino is looking around at his groom with a relaxed expression on his face. You should never tie your horse with the lead strap. You see the chain in this picture because Chino is being held while he is brushed.

Finally, you should take a hoof pick and clean each hoof. Cleaning the dirt from the under-portion of the hoof allows you to check for rocks and other objects that might bruise your horse while you ride.

To clean your horse's fore-foot, first lean gently against his shoulder to get him to shift his weight to his other fore-foot. Then place your hand on the back of the cannon and lift. Once the foot is raised, hold it in one hand and stand back from the horse a little ways so that he cannot lean against you. Very well-mannered animals will pick their feet up for you when you touch their cannon and say "pick-up your foot." Very poor-mannered horses will lean down hard on the hoof you are trying to lift. Sometimes a slap on the belly will make them behave. Some horses will raise their legs better if you pull on the back of the knee, or if you tap lightly on their cannon with the hoof pick. Many people squeeze the tendons on the back of the cannon to get the leg up. If the horse starts fighting or leaning after you have his leg raised, you can either reprimand him and hang on, or let go and try again.

You should clean all dirt and rocks from the sole and cleft of the frog. Be gentle: Do not damage the soft frog. However, you should try to get the foot clean. Work from the heel towards the toe of the hoof.

In order to pick up your horse's hind foot, stand beside him and push gently to get him to take his weight off the foot. Then, pull up and forward on the cannon. Stand back as you raise his foot in order to avoid getting struck should he jerk his leg forward or kick. Some horses will raise their foot for you as you approach, so don't automatically assume he is planning a kick if his foot goes up. If you always clean the feet in the same order—for example: right front, right rear, left front, left rear—your horse may learn the routine and raise his hooves for you as you approach them. This makes the job much easier.

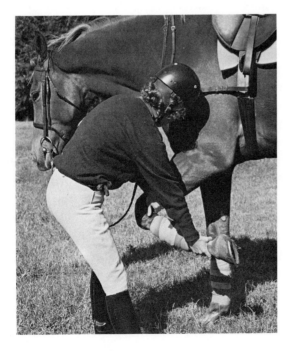

Figure 4–4. An easy way to lift a horse's fore-foot is this: pull forward on his knee and lift upward on his fetlock. Anrock raises his hoof even though he is standing untied in the riding area. Notice that he is wearing exercise bandages to protect his legs and shoes to protect his feet. Your horse may or may not need bandages or shoes. The rider is wearing a schooling helmet, breeches, and hunt boots. She has her gloves tucked into her pocket.

Figure 4–5. To pick up your horse's hind leg, pull forward and upward on his cannon. As you can see, horses can get their feet very dirty.

Figure 4–6. Animals that wear shoes are particularly bad about getting their feet packed with dirt. You should clean the hooves every day in order to avoid bruises and infections. The groom is pushing the pick toward the toe of the hoof while supporting the hoof in her other hand.

GROOMING AFTER YOU RIDE

The most important procedure after riding is to bring your horse to the stable cool. When you finish your lesson, ride him at a walk until he stops blowing and begins to feel cool to the touch. In your first lessons, your horse may never heat up, as you will be working him very lightly. In later lessons, you may need to walk him for fifteen minutes or so, so allow for this time when you plan your ride.

When you get to the barn, untack (remove the saddle and bridle) your horse immediately. Don't neglect him while you sit and talk with your friends. For the sake of his health, your horse should always come first. In hot weather, I wash my horses with the hose in order to remove the sweat and to cool their legs. Next I scrape them with the sweat scraper; and then I either turn them out to pasture or walk them and let them graze a little on the rope. In cool weather, I hose off their legs only, in order to prevent swelling and to help the horse cool. Then I rub the horse with a towel, and either walk him or turn him out. In very cold weather, I use no water. I rub the horses with a towel—back and legs. Then I walk them or turn them out. If the horse is sweaty in cold weather (mine rarely are), I cover him with a stable sheet or cooler and walk him until he is cool. Then I protect him from the wind until he is dry.

If my horse has worked very hard, or if I am afraid he might have strained himself, I use a body wash or leg wash on his legs instead of water. These washes cool and have a counter-irritant action: They discourage swelling and soreness. Always check your horse's feet after you ride: He might have picked up a stone. Check for saddle or girth sores, and for spots where the hair has rubbed off under the tack. Treat these with a good wound ointment. You should also check the legs for cuts and hot spots. Use a wound dressing on the cuts, and a liniment on any spots that look puffy or feel hot to the touch. Try to think what might have caused both problems, so that you can correct the situation.

Cleaning Tack

The term "tack" refers to the saddle, bridle, and, if you use one, a martingale. You should do a small amount of tack cleaning after each ride. Once a week or so, you should do a complete cleaning. Once a month, you should oil your tack.

After each ride, wash the bit with clean water in order to remove all saliva and the green traces of any little tidbits your horse managed to sneak while you weren't watching. If the bit is of a type that might rust, dry it with a soft, clean cloth. Lay the saddle pad and the girth or cinch with the damp faces up so they can dry. If you use a leather girth, you must wash it, along with any portions of the saddle that may have become sweaty. Use a sponge and glycerine saddle soap for this job.

Once a week, you should soap your saddle and bridle with glycerine soap. At this time, also check your leather halters, lead straps, and other leather items to see if they need cleaning. You will probably want to wash your saddle pad (brush felt and pressed pads) and your cloth girths.

Every month or so, you should take your tack apart and oil it. Undo all the straps of the bridle and take off the bit. Rub a small amount of oil into all joints in the leather, and onto the rough side of the leather of any portions that have become dry and stiff. Neatsfoot oil is the traditional potent: Several other oils that work better are on the market now. Neatsfoot oil has the disadvantage of turning the leather black and of rotting out cotton stitches.

Taking care of your horse and your equipment is a necessary part of horsemanship. It's true that you can learn to ride if someone else does all the dirty work. You can become a rider if you never do anything with your horse except ride him. However, you will not become a true, complete horseman or horsewoman unless you roll up your sleeves and groom, clean, and lunge. The more time you spend with your horse in the stable, the better you will understand him. Understanding your horse is essential to good horsemanship. Besides, most of us enjoy the stable care as much as we enjoy riding. You probably will too.

5 Problems with Your Horse in the Stable

If you choose your horse carefully, you will have no trouble with serious vices. However, no horse is perfect. Every animal will, sooner or later, do something which will distress or anger you. The purpose of this Chapter is to forewarn you, and to tell you how to cope.

NIPPING

Nipping is biting that is not hard enough to break the skin. Young horses and mares tend to be nippy no matter what you do. This is also true of ponies. Nipping is made worse by feeding your horse from your hand. He gets the idea that you taste good, and he wants to taste you again. When your horse nips, say "No!" in a mad voice and slap him on the neck. Do not hit his face—this action will make him shy about his head. If your animal is very persistent, then you must be persistent as well. Never let him nip without getting punished. Sooner or later he will stop.

KICKING

Many mares will kick at you with one leg when they get angry at you or when they are bothered. Young horses sometimes kick out of playfulness. Horses may kick when they are startled, or when fighting with another horse. If your horse kicks at you, you should punish him even if he doesn't connect.

Say "No!" in an angry voice, and slap your horse on the hip. Unless the horse is mean or soured, this will probably be enough. If the kick came because you startled the horse, then it is your fault, and you should not punish him. Otherwise, never let a kick go unpunished.

STEPPING ON YOUR FEET

I don't believe that horses step on your feet on purpose, simply because they cannot see their feet well enough to take a good aim. Usually, if your feet are stepped on, it's your fault for having them in the way. If this happens, push the horse to get him to take his weight off. Do not try to jerk your foot out from under his. You should not punish the horse. Some horses have a bad habit of always leaning towards you or edging towards you as they are being led. Naturally, they frequently step on your feet. You should make these horses stand farther away from you by jerking the lead strap, or by slapping them on the shoulder or belly.

THROWING FEED AROUND

This is irritating, as the horse will go to great pains to scatter his expensive feed all over the ground. The horse may throw it out of his bucket with his nose, stick his foot in the bucket and turn it over, or pick the bucket up in his mouth and shake it. Who knows why? The only correction is a feeder that is designed to prevent these problems, firmly mounted to the wall of the stall. Feeders with rims or feed-saver rings keep the feed where it belongs. Be sure to mount the feeder high enough to keep your wonderful beast from putting his feet in it and pulling it down.

PACING, PAWING, BREAKING OUT OF THE STALL, AND OTHER RESTLESSNESS

You may have these problems if you keep your horse alone, or if you have two horses in the stable and the other one goes out to work. Horses are very social creatures, and hate to be left by themselves. Unfortunately, only a few solutions exist. You can ignore your frantic animal, merely repairing damage to the stall and to your horse as it occurs. You can build a horse-proof stall. You can buy or otherwise obtain a third horse. Or, you can sell the troublesome beast and try to find one that is more settled in the stable.

EATING WOOD

Horses, like termites, frequently eat wooden boards. Some animals will literally eat their way out of stalls and paddocks. Many ideas are batted around as to why they do—perhaps the horse needs fiber in his diet. Perhaps he's bored. Maybe he likes the taste of the wood. Whatever the cause, horses will eat good-smelling wood like cedar, and soft wood such as pine, more often than the harder, less delicious smelling varieties. They rarely chew pressure-treated creosoted lumber.

Wood-eating is a habit you will want to firmly discourage. Besides eating your horse out of house and home, so to speak, the habit will also result in your horse suffering colic and more serious diseases of the digestive tract. Horses, unlike termites, cannot digest wood. In order to stop your horse from eating wood, you can paint or spray all exposed board surfaces with creosote. Or you can cover all the boards with a thin metal top. The only other solution is to rebuild your entire stable and paddock using treated lumber, or concrete blocks. Keeping hay in front of the animal sometimes does the trick. Do not rub salt in the wood. Rather than discouraging him, this will speed his eating. Horses love salt. A thick paste of hot pepper might do the trick—if you have several gallons of pepper.

EVADING BEING CAUGHT IN THE PASTURE

We discussed this problem briefly in Chapter 4, "How To Catch And Lead A Horse." Most horses will allow themselves to be caught from the pasture with little trouble, or with only token resistance. However, every so often you will come across a horse that is a real renegade. He may start running as soon as you enter the pasture, or he may allow you to get all the way to his head before he spins and trots away. Either way, it's aggravating. The cure is fairly simple and can be accomplished without trauma. It works best if you can put your horse in a small field by himself for a few days. Leave a halter on him, one which is adjusted so that he will be unlikely to catch his foot in it should he decide to scratch his face. With a really bad horse, you can leave four feet of rope attached to the halter. Don't leave more rope, or your horse will somehow manage to tie his legs together. Now, find a nice, big bucket and put feed in the bottom. Carry the feed bucket to the pasture gate. After you make sure your horse sees the bucket, slowly enter, carrying your bribe with you. Your horse will let you catch him before very long. (He may run you down in his eagerness for the feed!) Incidentally, this trick works best if the animal is hungry. After a couple of days, leave the bucket at the gate, and enter the pasture with a little feed in your hand. When you catch him, let your horse eat the feed. When he stops running from you (he may trot up to see you!) he is ready to return to the larger field and the company of other horses. You must carry feed with you in your hand from now on, or your horse will go back to his bad habits. It is better to buy a horse that can be caught without feed (See Part I).

RULES TO FOLLOW IN HANDLING PROBLEMS

In coping with problems with our horses, everyone is sometimes angry or frustrated. However, a good horseman or horsewoman avoids these actions:

Never Hit Your Horse about the Head. This will make him head shy—he won't let you touch his face or ears.

Never Scream. It's all right to raise your voice angrily, as long as you sound firm. But you must never sound frightened, shrill, or murderous.

Never Beat Your Horse with a Whip. If you must punish him for misbehavior, use the flat of your hand. Slapping makes a nice, angry sound without hurting your animal enough to make him afraid.

Never Lose Your Temper. You will do something your horse will later make you regret.

Never Panic. Your horse will follow your lead.

Never Chase Your Horse. He will run faster, and may kick you.

Never Allow Your Horse to Chase You. This is a dangerous game. If he catches you, you'll be sorry. He may knock you down, or kick at you. Never run from him. If he runs at you, stand still and wave your arms. He will back off.

Never Startle Your Horse. Don't wave strange objects, or make loud, unusual sounds, or quick, threatening movements around your horse. Horses panic easily, and react violently when afraid.

If You Do Punish Your Horse, Don't Delay. Horses have very short memories. They must be punished within seconds of the infraction if they are to get the message you wish to convey.

Hopefully, you will never have any of these problems with your horse. However, you should not be surprised or upset if your horse does give you a little grief. Horses are living creatures, and as such they have their moods, and their faults. The problems I discuss in this chapter are really fairly common with all horses. If you follow the rules and advice I give, you will be able to cope and to correct your horse.

In the next chapter, you will begin the actual riding lessons. After you select your horse, you might wish to begin riding right away. Or you might prefer to take a few days to get familiar with the animal before you get on his back. Either way, I'm sure that you will soon find that the pleasures of riding and working with your horse make all the little problems unimportant in your eyes.

TEST: PART II, CHAPTERS 3–5

1. True or false:
    a. To catch a horse from a box stall, stand at the door and call him.
    b. Always carry a feed bucket with you when you go to catch your horse from the pasture.
    c. Attach the lead strap or tie rope to the ring at the bottom of the halter.
    d. Lead from the left side of your horse.
    e. Always wrap the lead strap around your hand. This gives you a better grip.
    f. When you come to a gate, open it all the way in order to give your horse plenty of room.
    g. If your horse refuses to follow you, leave him in the pasture.
2. List five safety rules for tying your horse.
3. List three things you should always do when you groom your horse before riding.
4. Multiple choice:
    a. The most important procedure after riding is
        (1) let your horse drink clean water.
        (2) bring your horse to the stable cool.
        (3) wash your horse with a hose.
    b. When you get to the barn
        (1) ask your friends what you did wrong in your lesson.
        (2) tie your horse in the shade.
        (3) immediately untack your horse.
    c. Use a body wash
        (1) to get your horse clean.

(2) to make your horse smell better.

(3) to help your horse cool without soreness.

  d. You should

    (1) clean your tack once a month.

    (2) oil your tack once a week.

    (3) clean your tack once a week.

5. Describe the cure for each of the following problems:

  a. Kicking

  b. Nipping

  c. Stepping on your feet

  d. Eating wood

  e. Being hard to catch in the pasture.

6. List nine rules to follow in coping with problems with your horse.

LEARN-
ING
TO RIDE

This section covers the actual riding lessons. In Chapter 6 we discuss the introductory lessons. These lessons teach the most elementary riding skills. More advanced, but still basic, riding skills are covered in Chapter 7. Except for Lesson 1 in Chapter 6, which takes from 30–60 minutes, and for Lesson 12 in Chapter 7, which lasts for 60–180 minutes, each lesson is designed to be learned in practice sessions of one hour. You should work toward accomplishing the skills described within this time. Chapter 7 ends with final tests of your riding skills and knowledge. Answers are in the Appendix.

6 Introduction to Riding

Each lesson in this chapter is outlined, and then explained. All four are designed as introductions to their subjects. Therefore, you should aim for only minimum proficiency in each skill. It is not necessary for you to mount with skill and grace (Lesson 1) in order to proceed to Lesson 2. As long as you understand the theory of the exercises, and are able to do them with some small degree of success, you should advance.

Both English and Western riders should do all the exercises in this chapter. While it is true that Western horsemen do not post, posting is a valuable skill that will improve your general riding ability. Western riders should learn the elementary posting taught here.

I assume that you wish to learn to ride correctly and well. However, if you want only an introduction to riding, take the lessons in this chapter, including Lesson 4A. Students who want to learn more than simply hanging on at different speeds should skip Lesson 4A, and take all the lessons in Chapter 7.

The lessons in Chapter 6 should be ridden with a snaffle bit or a mild curb. Do not carry a crop unless absolutely necessary (see Lesson 6). In Chapter 7, Western riders may use a Western curb bit. Do not go on to Chapter 7 until you have passed all the tests at the end of Chapter 6.

As a general rule, allow yourself from one to three hours to learn each lesson. You should practice in sessions of one hour. Don't tire yourself and your horse by trying to crowd too much

81

into too short a time. For best results, ride every day. You should plan to practice at least four hours a week if you wish to learn with any degree of success.

You are your own teacher, and thus your own judge. And you must grade your own progress. Be fair to yourself, and you will develop good riding skills.

LESSON 1:
THE WALK (30–60 MINUTES)

A / Tack your horse.	5–10 minutes
B / Mount. Take the reins.	5–10 minutes
C / Do starts and stops at the walk.	5–10 minutes
D / Do simple turns at the walk.	5–10 minutes
E / Study position at the walk.	5–10 minutes
F / Do the rising position at the walk.	5–10 minutes
G / Dismount.	

A / Tack Your Horse

SADDLE

To saddle your horse, follow this procedure:

1. Stand on the near side and lay the pad gently onto your horse's back. The pad should cover the back portion of the withers, and most or all of the back. Many people recommend laying the pad forward of the correct position, and then sliding it back into place. This action smooths the horse's hair and helps prevent saddle sores.

2. In an English saddle, check to see that the stirrups are run up the leathers. Lay the girth over the seat of the saddle. In a Western saddle, lay the cinch over the seat of the saddle, and hook the off (or right) stirrup on the horn. (The left stirrup is called the "near" stirrup.) These actions keep the girth or cinch from becoming hung beneath

Figure 6-1. This is an example of the properly tacked horse. The saddle is straight and placed so that the girth is one hand's width behind Anrock's elbow. The bridle is neat, with the straps tucked into the keepers. The bit rests correctly in the corners of his mouth. Anrock is wearing an Italian jumping saddle with an elastic-end, leather, chafeless girth. The pad is quilted cotton. He has a hunt bridle with a German snaffle bit. The chain you see is from the lead strap his handler is using for control.

the saddle, and keep the off stirrup from banging into your horse's side.

3. Swing the saddle upwards until it is suspended over your mount's back. Lower it gently into place. Never throw the saddle roughly onto your horse. You might frighten or injure him.

Figure 6-2. Here Anrock is tacked improperly. His saddle is too far back, and the stirrup is run up the wrong side of the leather. The bridle is not neat; the straps are out of the keepers. You can see how unhappy Anrock looks. He is wearing a full hunt bridle in this picture.

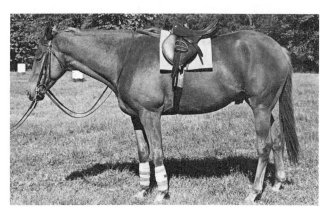

4. Shake the saddle a little until it settles into the correct position. The saddle should sit so that the pommel is over his withers, and so the girth or cinch will tighten in the heart or girth of your horse. A hand's width should stretch between your horse's elbow and the front edge of the girth. If the saddle is too far forward, slide it gently back. If it is behind the correct point, take it off and try again. Don't pull the saddle forward, as this will comb the horse's hair against its direction of growth, and predispose your horse to saddle sores.

5. Once the saddle is settled, lift the pad into the underside of the pommel. This action helps prevent sores on the withers.

6. Lower the cinch or girth from the off side. In a Western saddle, also lower the off stirrup. Check to make sure that the pad is not misplaced, or that the saddle twisted in some manner, on the off side.

7. Step back to the near side. Draw the girth or cinch under your horse. On a Western saddle, use only the front cinch (should your saddle have two cinches). Tie up the rear cinch, or take it off. Tighten the cinch with a cinch knot (see Figure 6-3). This knot is easy to tighten, and will not slip while you ride. To tie the cinch knot, follow these steps:

1. Place the free end of the latigo (leather strap on the saddle) through the ring on the cinch.

2. Bring the free end of the latigo up to the saddle and slip it through the rigging ring (the big ring on the side of the saddle).

3. Draw the free end of the latigo out the left side of the rigging ring. Cross it over, and tuck it back through the rigging ring on the right side of the ring.

4. Tighten the cinch.

5. Finally, tuck the free end of the latigo through the loop where the latigo crosses over the rigging ring. Pull it tight. You now have your cinch secured with a cinch knot.

Some Western saddles have holes punched in them so you can buckle the cinch in place. You naturally will not need to tie a cinch knot if your saddle is made like this. Merely use the kind of cinch that has buckles on the ends, instead of rings. Other Western saddles buckle to the cinch on one side, and tie with a cinch knot on the other. Whichever type of saddle you use, make sure your cinch is tight, but not too tight. It is very easy to tighten a cinch too much. You should be able to get two fingers between the cinch and your horse's side. In an English saddle, run the billets through the top part of the buckles on the girth

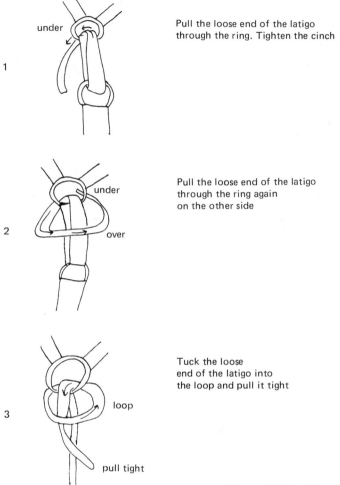

Pull the loose end of the latigo
through the ring. Tighten the cinch

Pull the loose end of the latigo
through the ring again
on the other side

Tuck the loose
end of the latigo into
the loop and pull it tight

Figure 6–3. The cinch knot.

and pull tight. You may use any two of the three billets, but you should use the same two billets on each side of the saddle. Tighten both billets to the same hole. When the girth or cinch is tightened, you should be able to get two fingers between it and the horse's side. Do not draw the girth up too tightly.

8. To adjust the length of your stirrups, stand on the near side of your horse. Place the tips of your fingers on the seat jockey (Western) or the stirrup bar (English). Pull the fender or leather along your right arm. The stirrup should fit snuggly into your right arm pit. Actually, this method gives only a crude estimate of correct length. It works

Figure 6–4. The cinch knot. It should be tightened before you mount.

Figure 6–5. The billets should be through the top of the girth buckles and drawn up evenly, as shown. You may use any two billets as long as you use the same two on each side of the saddle. The small flap on the billets should be drawn down over the buckles in order to protect the saddle from wear.

well only if your arms and legs are average in proportion. You should check the stirrup length again after you are in the saddle. When you sit as deeply in the saddle as you can, with your legs hanging relaxed, the stirrups should be on a level with your ankle. If Western stirrups

Figure 6–6. After tightening the girth or cinch, ''shake hands'' with your horse. This action draws the skin tight under the girth and helps prevent sores. Anrock is wearing a breast plate to keep the saddle from sliding back out of position. Breast plates are made for both English and Western saddles, but most horses don't need them. You will need one if your saddle won't stay in place while you ride.

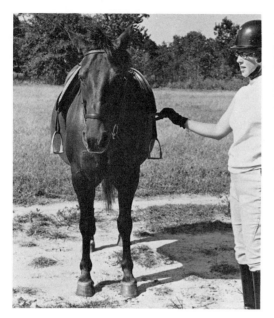

Figure 6–7. Check to make sure both stirrups are the same length before you mount. It's very hard to tell this from on top of your horse. Chocolate is wearing her right stirrup several inches shorter than her left stirrup. If you tried to ride like this, you would have a tendency to lean in the saddle.

Figure 6–8. In English saddles, the stirrup should hit you on your ankle when you sit with your feet out. Western stirrups should be about one inch longer. Chocolate is wearing a hunt bridle with a hunt snaffle and a dropped-nose band adjusted above the bit. The reins are knotted to keep the bight out of the way. Sometimes this is necessary with long reins and little horses. There is a crop peeking out from under the saddle. You can put the crop under the saddle to mount, but you shouldn't leave it there while you ride. It might fall out and get lost.

need adjustment, dismount to do it. In English saddles, you can adjust the stirrups while mounted. Also, you should stand in front of your horse to check on whether both stirrups are the same length. Having one stirrup shorter than the other is a common fault in beginners.

BRIDLE

Bridling is a fairly simple exercise, if you do it correctly. Done wrong, it can take the better part of an hour. To bridle your horse, proceed as follows:

Figure 6-9. You can tighten the girth of an English saddle from on top of your horse. Unfortunately, you must dismount to tighten most Western cinches. When you tighten the girth, slide your leg forward. Don't push it back into your horse's side.

Figure 6-10. Keep your foot in the stirrups when you adjust English stirrups from on top of your horse. Simply pull the leather buckle out and make the desired changes. Larger-numbered holes mean shorter stirrups. Be sure to put the buckle back under the skirt when you finish.

1. Stand on the near side of the animal. Remove his halter, and refasten it so that it is around his neck. Your horse thus remains tied, and cannot wander away.

2. Place the reins over his head, so that they fall around his neck. Thus, they will be out of your way while you bridle.

3. Hold the crown of the bridle in your right hand, the bit in your left. If at all possible, slide your right hand up so that it rests between your mount's ears. This action will keep his head down; how-

ever, some horses are too tall for you to do this easily, and others will strongly resist you. For these animals, you must place your right hand on their foreheads, above their eyes.

4. Bring the bit up so that it touches your horse's mouth. With luck, he will open his mouth, and allow you to draw the bridle up until the bit is in his mouth. If he refuses to open for the bit, do not try to ram in the cold metal. Instead, slip your thumb gently into the side of his mouth. You are in no danger, as your horse has no teeth near the corners of his lips. You need not press: Horses dislike the taste of human hands. When he tries to spit out your finger, draw the bit into his mouth.

5. As you place the bit in his mouth, raise your right hand to the horse's ears. Then, with your left hand, pull each ear gently under the crown piece. Do not be rough, as his ears are very tender.

6. Fasten the throat latch. You should be able to get your fist between this strap and your horse's throttle. The only purpose of the throat latch is to keep your mount from rubbing his bridle off when he scratches his ears. It need not, and should not, be drawn tightly. If this strap is too tight, he will not be able to breathe freely.

7. Fasten the curb chain, if your bridle has one. First, twist the chain until it lies flat. There should be no kinks! Now, hook the chain so that you can get three fingers flat between it and the horse's chin. Hooked too tight, the chain is very severe. Hooked too loosely, it has no effect at all.

8. Buckle the noseband. This strap should fall about an inch below your mount's jawbone, and should be pulled only tight enough to make it look neat. You should be able to get a whole hand, flat, between the noseband and your animal's nose.

Figure 6–11. To bridle your horse, first slip off the halter and hook it around your horse's neck. You should saddle him before you put on the bridle. The bridle should be the last thing you put on your horse before you ride and the first thing you take off him when you finish your ride.

Figure 6–12. Most horses will cooperate with you if you bridle them correctly. Place your right hand between the ears and raise the bit gently into the mouth. Slip your thumb between the lips if the horse won't open his mouth, but don't try to force his mouth open. He'll open it in a moment if you're patient.

Figure 6–13. Next, gently pull his ears under the crown piece.

9. If your bridle has a dropped noseband, adjust the noseband either directly below, or about a half-inch above, the bit. Make sure you do not pinch your horse's lips between the noseband and the bit. As the purpose of this device is to prevent your mount from throwing his mouth wide open—and not to buckle his mouth shut!—you should not draw it on too tightly. Make sure you can get two fingers, laid flat, between the noseband and the top of your horse's nose.

Figure 6–14. Carefully fasten all the buckles. On most English bridles, the throat latch is the only buckle you fasten and unfasten in bridling and unbridling. Don't undo the buckles on the cheeks. Some Western bridles have a throat latch, while others simply pull over the ears.

Figure 6-15. Finally, remove the halter from around your horse's neck. Straighten the bridle. You are now ready to ride.

10. Check the adjustment of the bridle, if necessary. The bit should fit snugly against your horse's lips. If it hangs either too high or too low, it will be more severe than you wish.

11. Make sure all the keepers (the little loops on the bridle) are in place, holding the loose ends of the straps.

MARTINGALE

Finally (if you use one), you should check the adjustment of the standing martingale. The neck strap of the martingale should be adjusted so that you can slip one fist between it and your mount's neck. If it is too tight, it will cut off his breathing; if it is too loose, he may hang a leg in the martingale. Western tie-downs frequently don't have neck-straps. This is extremely dangerous! If your tie-down came without a neck strap, make one out of some old leather, or from a bit of rope. If your horse catches his leg over the tie-down, he will fall, possibly breaking all sorts of things—including your neck.

The martingale should be tightened just enough to keep your horse from raising his head too high. Get him to hold his head in a natural position, and shorten the strap until it pulls loosely into a straight line. See Figures 6-16a, b and c for adjustments of the martingale. The martingale should then be firmly attached to the noseband of the bridle. Do not use a martingale with a dropped noseband, unless you also use a regular noseband. Fasten the martingale to the regular noseband.

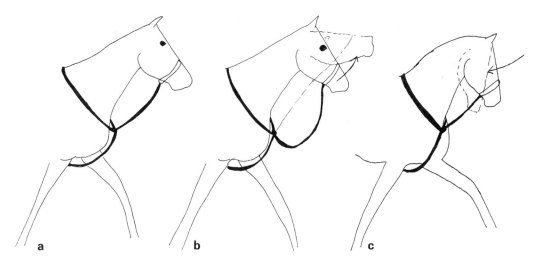

a   b   c

Figure 6–16a. The standing martingale, when correctly adjusted, allows the horse to carry his head in a relaxed position.

Figure 6–16b. If the martingale is too loose, the horse can raise his head too high. Adjusted like this, the martingale has no function.

Figure 6–16c. If the martingale is too tight, it forces the horse to carry his head in a cramped position. The horse will be uncomfortable and may overflex or rear.

B / Mounting

MOUNTING FROM THE SIDE

Mounting is the same in both English and Western riding. The procedure follows:

1. Always work from the near side of your horse. First, check the tightness of the girth or cinch. Frequently the girth will loosen mysteriously between the time you first take it up and the time you mount. This is because your horse will have let out the air he sucked into his lungs when you put the saddle on his back. If you mount without checking the cinch, you may find the saddle slipping around the horse's barrel.

2. Stand on the left side of your horse, facing the saddle.

3. Gather your reins in your left hand, making sure that both reins are the same length. Now place your left hand on the horse's withers, and shorten your reins until there is a straight line from your

hand to the bit. If you leave the reins loose, your horse might walk off at the wrong time. If you have only one rein tight, he will probably spin. With both reins too tight, however, he will tend to move backwards. You want a light touch—just enough to keep him still.

4. Grab a hunk of mane in your left hand, without letting go of the reins! Don't be afraid of hurting your mount. Horses have no nerves in the roots of their mane hairs.

5. With your right hand, place your left foot in the stirrup. Turn your toe down, so that you will not goose your horse in the side.

6. Grab the pommel of the saddle with your right hand. You may grab the horn in a Western saddle. Do not grab the cantle, as this will pull the saddle out of place, and may warp the tree of a huntseat saddle.

7. Hop on your left foot and draw yourself up so that your weight is supported by the left stirrup, and by both your hands. You should not stay here too long, as your weight in the stirrup may draw the saddle to one side.

8. Swing your right leg over your horse's croup, being careful not to kick him in the flank.

Figure 6–17. The first step in mounting is to pull the stirrups down on both sides of the saddle. Western riders should also check both sides of the saddle to make sure the saddle is on straight.

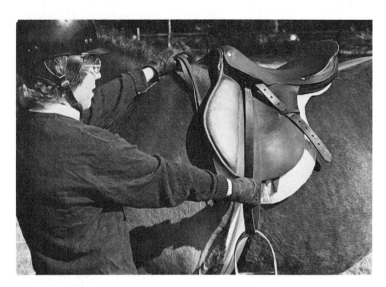

Figure 6–18. Next, gather the reins in your left hand. Both reins should be equally tight, but not tight enough to make your horse step backward. Standing by your mount's shoulder, turn the stirrup toward you.

Figure 6–19. Your left hand should hold the reins and a little bit of mane. This is true for both English and Western riders. Place your left foot in the stirrup and grab the saddle with your right hand. You should grab the saddle pommel, horn, leather, or fender, whichever is easiest for you. Do not grab the cantle of the saddle.

9. Settle gently into the saddle. Don't drop suddenly. How would you like your weight thudding onto your back? Your horse won't like it either.

10. Take your right stirrup. You should try to do this without looking down, or without helping yourself with your hand. However, in the first few lessons, you may need to cheat a little.

MOUNTING FROM THE FRONT

The form of mounting outlined above is called "mounting from the side." This is the only correct way to mount in Western horsemanship. In English riding, however, people sometimes mount from the front. I always do, as I am short, and mounting

Figure 6–20. Give a little hop and push yourself up, swinging your leg high over your horse's rump. Be very careful not to kick him while you mount!

Figure 6–21. Settle gently down into the saddle. Don't land like a sack of potatoes, as you will hurt your horse's back. Place your right foot in the stirrup and put both hands on the reins before you allow your horse to walk away.

from the front is easier for me. To follow this procedure, you need change the above outline only in point number "2":

2. Stand by your horse's left shoulder, facing his croup. If you are too short to reach the pommel of the saddle, you may pull up by grabbing the stirrup leather. Do not pull on the flap, as this will cause the saddle to become misshapen. As a final note, never mount from the rear, facing your horse's head. Your horse might bring a hind leg up and kick you in the back. Also, if he should take even one step forward, he will get away from you.

HOLDING THE REINS

In later lessons, Western riders will learn another way to hold the reins. For now, however, all students should hold the reins as shown. This method gives you maximum control of your horse in beginning lessons. Briefly, the reins should enter the bottom of your hands, so that your little finger is closer to the bit, and your thumb is closer to the buckle, or free, end of the reins. Make sure that both reins are the same length. In these early lessons, you should ride with a little, but not too much, slack. Let your fingers circle the reins loosely; they should close, but not grip tightly. Put the free end of the rein under your thumb. Now, relax and let your hands turn so that your knuckles are slanted at the same angle as the shoulders of your mount. Keep your wrists straight, but not stiff.

C / Starts and Stops at the Walk

THE CORRECT POSITION AT THE HALT

Though position is not necessarily the most important part of riding, few people can learn to ride well with a poor position in the saddle. From the very first lesson, you should be constantly monitoring your position. It is all too easy to develop bad habits which will be hard to break later. Correct position at the halt is exactly the same for all three styles of riding.

Figure 6–22. Both English and Western riders should hold the reins as illustrated for the first lessons. The reins should come from your horse's mouth, through the bottom of your hands, and out under your thumbs. You can slip the reins between your little fingers and your ring fingers if you desire. Hold the reins loosely, using your thumbs to keep them in your hands. Put the bight, or loose ends of the reins, together on one side of your horse's neck.

Sit in the deepest part of the saddle. In an English saddle, this should be in the exact center. Your weight should be distributed over the points of your buttocks (the two little bones in your seat) and your crotch. You should feel the saddle under your crotch. If you don't, you are sitting too much on your rear. You should also feel the saddle under the points of your buttocks: Sitting too far forward is also a fault. Your back should be straight, not slumped. Hold your head up, and keep your eyes forward. Your legs should be positioned so that the stirrup leathers, or fenders, fall perpendicular to the ground. Your toes should fall in a line with your knees, and point slightly outward, in an angle that is comfortable for you. Your heels should flex downwards, and not be drawn up into your horse's side. Keep your knees as close to the saddle as you can. Later, your thighs will flatten and develop, making leg position easier for you. Your elbows should rest lightly at your sides, and your hands should be slightly above your mount's withers. Keep your hands five-to-ten inches apart, depending upon the thickness of your horse's neck. Your hands should be as far apart as his neck is wide at the thickest point.

Figure 6–23. This is the correct position in the English saddle. The rider is sitting up straight, with her shoulders back and her elbows at her side. Her buttocks are pushed out behind her. Her knees are against the saddle, and her toes are even with her knees. Her heels are down. Her hands are over her horse's withers, in front of the saddle. She is riding in a German-style, Argentine saddle in this picture. Note that Anrock is too big for this rider. Her feet come up above the bottom of his barrel. The saddle is also too big. Both of these factors can cause her trouble as she takes her lessons.

Figure 6–24. This is the correct position for Western riders. In these beginning lessons, you will hold the reins with both hands. Otherwise, you would sit like the rider here. Sit up straight, with your shoulders back and your buttocks pushed out behind you. Your toes should be even with, or slightly in front of, your knees. Your heels should be down. Your knees should be against the saddle, and your elbows should be by your sides.

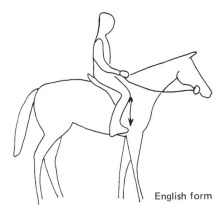

English form

Figure 6–25. Position at the halt and walk: English form
1. Hands should be over and slightly in front of the withers. They should be separated by 5 to 9 inches and turned at the same angle as the angle of the horse's shoulders.
2. The body of the rider should be vertical, with the back straight.
3. The heels should be down and the toes turned out at a relaxed angle.
4. There should be a straight line from the rider's knee to toes.
5. The eyes should be up and the shoulders back.
6. The rider should feel comfortable and relaxed.

EXERCISES TO HELP YOUR POSITION

You can do these exercises before you ride to help limber your body:

1. Balance a book on your head. This helps your posture in the saddle.

2. Stand with your toes on a step, and bounce. This stretches your ankles and strengthens your calves.

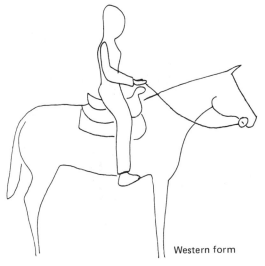

Western form

Figure 6–26. Position at the halt and walk: Western form
1. The rider should sit straight in the saddle.
2. The toes should be even with or slightly to the front of the knees.
3. The heels should be lower than the toes.
4. The rider should sit deep in the saddle.
5. The eyes should be up and the shoulders back.
6. The rider should feel comfortable and relaxed.

Figure 6–27. Many beginning riders are too stiff, like the rider in this picture. She is leaning forward, with her heels drawn up and her arms out straight. If Chocolate were moving, she would be bouncing. She is riding in a German jumping saddle.

Figure 6–28. Here is the same rider in the same saddle showing us another common way beginners ride. She is sitting on her buttocks, with her heels up. If Chocolate were moving she would be bouncing.

Figure 6–29. Beginners soon learn that if you brace off the stirrups you don't bounce. However, if your horse does anything unexpected, you do fall off.

MECHANICS OF THE WALK

The walk of the horse is a four-beat gait, meaning that each foot strikes the ground individually. At every moment, two or three feet are on the ground, and one or two feet are in the air. (For the sequence, see Figure 6-34.) Unlike the other gaits (trot, gallop, or canter), at no time during the walk are all four legs off the ground. Therefore, the walk is a smooth, easy gait to ride. The motion in the horse's back is a forward and backward rocking movement.

HOW TO START THE WALK

To make your horse walk, first make sure you are not pulling on the reins. The reins should be fairly loose. Next, tap with your heels on your horse's sides—do not pull your knees away from the saddle! It helps if you also say "Walk." Many horses are familiar with voice commands. Do not kick your mount too

Figure 6–30. When you walk your horse, your form should be the same as at the halt. Let your mount have a loose rein and try to relax so that your back moves with his motion. This rider has her heels turned in too far. Your foot should turn out at a relaxed angle, but no more than 45 degrees. Anrock is wearing a foam pad with extra padding under the seat of the saddle. You can buy foam very cheaply at discount stores. The extra padding raises the back of the saddle so that the deepest part of the seat is in the center of the saddle. You cannot balance correctly in an English saddle if you are sitting on the cantle.

hard, as he may trot if you give him a heavy blow. First give a light touch with your heels. If he doesn't walk, hit him a little more sharply with your heels.

HOW TO STOP THE WALK

To make your horse stop, draw the reins backwards until they tighten slightly against his mouth. You should not need to pull your hands more than a couple of inches. If your hands wind up behind your back, you are holding your reins too loosely. If you see your horse open his mouth, or throw up his head, or tuck his chin down to his chest, you are pulling too hard—relax your pull. You should hold a light, steady pressure

Figure 6–31. To stop, pull your hand backward until the reins make contact with your horse's mouth. You may hold onto the pommel if you desire. You should never hesitate to grab the pommel or the saddle horn while you are learning.

Figure 6–32. Sometimes beginners try to stop by bracing on the stirrups. This is a serious mistake, as your horse will pull against your hands. Be careful never to do this.

4

3

2

1

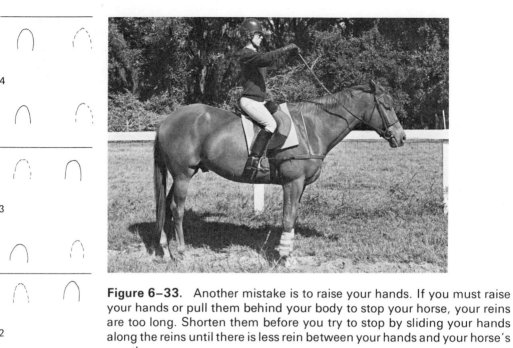

Figure 6–33. Another mistake is to raise your hands. If you must raise your hands or pull them behind your body to stop your horse, your reins are too long. Shorten them before you try to stop by sliding your hands along the reins until there is less rein between your hands and your horse's mouth.

against his mouth until he stops (about a second, if you do it correctly). As soon as your mount stops, relax the reins, and pat his neck. These actions relax both you and your horse. Sometimes, you might not pull hard enough. Make sure both reins are pulled into a straight line. It helps if you say "Whoa!"

PRACTICE

To practice starts and stops, merely mount inside the ring and begin. Let your horse walk freely the first few times, as you concentrate on getting a good, smooth start and a smooth, relaxed stop. Then, continue to practice starts and stops while you also study the rest of this lesson.

Figure 6–34. Sequence of legs at the walk.

D / Simple Turns at the Walk

The simplest turn you can do is accomplished with the aid of the leading rein. To use the leading rein, merely pull your hand out a few inches from its normal position, and lead the horse into the

Figure 6–35. The track is a path around the ring. If your ring has a track, you should try to ride in it.

Figure 6–36. Anrock is turning at the trot for the right leading rein. You can turn your horse with the leading rein at any speed. He should turn his whole body and not just his head. Be sure to carry your leading hand well to the side. Pull out, not back.

turn. For example, to make a right turn, take your right hand six inches to the right. Note that the rein must be short enough for this action to reach your horse's mouth! Also, it is vital that you do not unconsciously interfere with your left hand, which will want to follow your right. Do not pull your left hand to the right. If you have trouble using only one hand at a time, place the offending hand against the withers to hold it still. At no time should your hand cross the mid-line of your mount's neck.

To practice simple turns, make your horse walk around the inside of the ring just to the right or left of the rail. If a track, or path, exists, walk in it. Every so often you should turn and walk across the ring. When you reach the other side, you may continue in the same direction, or reverse direction. For a sequence of simple turns, see Figure 6-39. Also practice starts and stops, and practice your position at the walk.

Figure 6–37.   Most beginners make the mistake of moving both hands when they try to turn. Don't do this, as your horse won't turn right if you pull on the left rein. Put your left hand on your horse's neck so the left rein will stay loose.

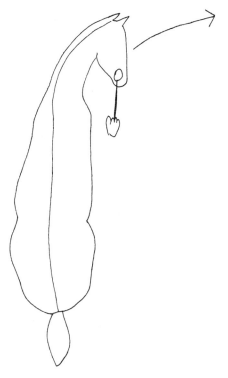

Figure 6–38.   The leading rein.

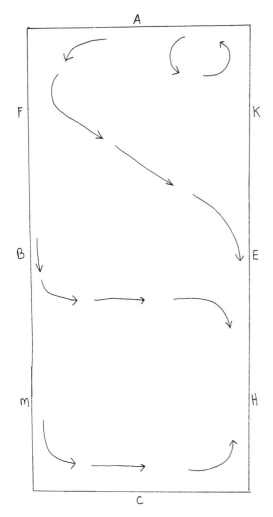

A

F

K

B

E

m

H

C

Figure 6–39. Simple turns.

E / Position at the Walk

Your position at the walk should be exactly the same as your position at the halt, with one exception. At the walk, your horse is moving; therefore, you must also move. Do not hold your body stiff. You should move backwards and forwards from the waist so that you absorb the horse's motion in your pelvic region and your legs. Your upper body should remain still. Also, notice that at a walk your horse nods his head. With each stride his head goes up and down. Eventually, you must learn to follow that motion with your hands, so that your hands will be supple and responsive to his mouth. Practice moving your hands with the motion of his neck. Your arms should move forward and backward from your shoulders and elbows.

An exercise you can do on the ground to help limber your back is the "hula hoop." This device is excellent for developing the suppleness that you need to ride the walk—and later, the sitting trot and canter. To check your position in the saddle, stop your horse. Drop the reins and raise your hands high above your head. This action will get all the slumping out of your back, and put you upon the correct bones in your buttocks and crotch.

F / Rising Position at the Walk

The rising position is an excellent exercise to develop correct leg position, and to muscle up your thighs and calves. However, it only works if you do it right!

First push your weight down into the stirrups, lowering your heels as much as possible. Then lean forward and raise your buttocks out of the saddle. Your back should be straight,

Figure 6–40a. In the correct rising position, you should lean forward until your seat is completely out of the saddle. Your back should be straight, your heels down, and your hands down on your horse's neck.

Figure 6–40b. Western riders also lean forward to take the rising position. Since the stirrups are longer and the saddle has a horn, these riders do not lean as far forward as do English riders. The rider in the picture is in good form. Her heels are down, her legs are in against the saddle, her back is straight, and her seat is just slightly out of the saddle. She is hanging on to Chocolate's mane for support, something you will need to do to your horse's mane for some time.

Figure 6–41. Beginners commonly pitch forward and bring their heels up. You should try to avoid this, as it throws you off balance. It also annoys your horse.

Figure 6–42. Another mistake is stiffness. To benefit from this exercise, you must bend your knees so that your thighs are pressing into the saddle. Also, be careful not to arch or hollow your back.

with a slight hollow at your waist, Eventually, you should be able to hold this position without using your hands for support, at all gaits. For now, it's all right to brace against your horse's neck or pull on the mane, if necessary. Use your thighs as much as possible, as this is the only good exercise for building your thigh muscles. Remember to keep your heels down!

Practice at the halt until you feel you have the position correct. Then practice at the walk, taking short breaks to review the earlier sections of this lesson.

G / Dismounting

In this first lesson, correct form in dismounting is not really important. I'm going to discuss it now merely for convenience. Don't be concerned if it takes you a while to learn to dismount smoothly. Follow these steps:

1. Gather the reins in your left hand, and place this hand on the withers. Grab a little of your horse's mane.

2. Take your right foot from the stirrup.

3. Place your right hand on the pommel of the saddle. You may use the horn in a Western saddle.

4. Swing your right leg over your horse's croup.

5. Stand briefly in your left stirrup.

6. If you are riding Western, step down and remove your left foot. Walk to your horse's head.

7. If you are riding English, put your weight on your hands and kick your left foot from the stirrup. Drop gently to the ground, and walk to your horse's head.

LESSON 2: THE TROT

Tack and mount.

Review Lesson 1, paying particular at-   5 minutes tention to starts, stops, and turns.

Figure 6–43. The first step in dismounting, English or Western style, is to gather your reins into your left hand. Put your left hand on your horse's neck and your right hand on the pommel or horn of your saddle.

Figure 6–44. Swing your right leg high, so that you do not kick your mount. If you kick him, he may jump forward.

Figure 6–45. Stand briefly in the stirrup, supporting your weight on your hands. Western riders should slowly step down, being careful not to dig their mounts with their toes as they descend.

Figure 6–46. The English rider should kick his left foot free and lower himself to the ground. You may slide down sideways to avoid scratching the saddle with your belt buckle, if you desire.

Figure 6–47. Loosen the girth or cinch as soon as you get off. English riders should run up the stirrups to keep them from banging the horse's side. When you loosen the girth, you reward your mount for a job well done.

Review the rising position at the walk. Check your form at the sitting walk.	**10 minutes**
A / Do starts and stops at the trot.	**5 minutes**
B / Do the sitting trot, and turns at the sitting trot.	**20 minutes**
C / Do the rising position at the trot. Dismount.	**20 minutes**

A / Starts and Stops at the Trot

MECHANICS OF THE TROT

The trot is a two-beat gait. The diagonal pairs of legs work together (for the sequence, see Figure 6–48). First the right fore and the left hind legs will be on the ground, with the other two legs in the air. Then the right fore and left hind legs lift. For a moment, no legs are touching the ground! Finally, the left fore and right hind legs strike the ground, and a slight shock is

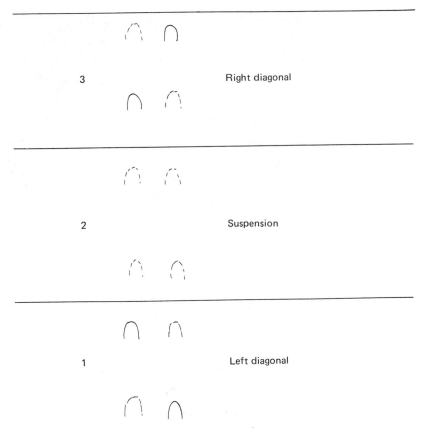

Figure 6–48. Sequence of the legs at the trot.

transmitted to the rider. The right fore and left hind legs are called the right diagonal pair; the left diagonal pair consists of the left fore and right hind legs. When you ride the trot, you experience what feels like a series of jolts.

HOW TO START THE TROT

The first few times you trot you should grab the mane or the pommel of the saddle. This action will steady you as you learn to adapt to the new sensation. Continue to hold the reins in both hands. Merely grab some of the horse's mane or the pommel with one hand without letting go of the rein. To make your horse trot, tap with your heels. Never take your knees off the saddle! Tap only hard enough to make him trot, then be sure to lower your heels out of his side. Do not hang on with your heels! You might make him buck or run if you do. Hang on with your hands until you learn to balance and go with the motion of your mount. Some horses will trot if you say "Trot!" or if you click with your tongue.

HOW TO STOP THE TROT

To make your horse walk, try saying "Walk!" If he doesn't respond, you will need to pull back on the reins. You may let go of the mane and pull with both hands, or you may take both reins in one hand to pull. You should need only a short pull in order to establish contact with your horse's mouth. If you need to bring your hand too far back to tighten the reins, your reins are too long. Once you have contact, hold it lightly until he stops trotting and begins to walk. Do not force him to halt completely. As soon as your horse walks, relax the reins and pat his neck. You should need no more pressure to bring your horse from a trot to a walk than you needed to make him halt from a walk.

PRACTICE

Practice starting and stopping from a trot until you feel more or less relaxed about the whole thing. Let your mount go where he wants at first. As soon as you feel capable, you should practice holding him to the track. Use the leading rein. You can hold on with one hand and direct your horse with the other, if necessary.

B / The Sitting Trot, with Turns

POSITION AT THE SITTING TROT

Riding the sitting trot is easiest if your horse is smooth-gaited and slow. However, you can learn to ride on any animal if you practice your position and develop your suppleness. The sitting trot is a very important exercise for building your riding

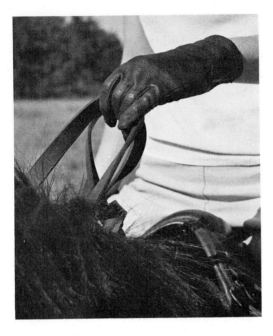

Figure 6–49. If you want to, you can hold the reins in one hand and grab your horse's mane or the saddle with your other hand. Cross the reins so that one enters under your little finger and the other enters under your thumb. This way you can easily go back to using both hands on the reins at any time. Make sure the reins are the same length.

skills. Your position should be the same one you took at the halt and at the walk. Do not lean forward, or slump backwards. Keep your head up, your shoulders back, and your heels down. Don't allow your feet to slip forward or backwards. Your toes should be lined up with your knees. You must absorb the shock of the trot with your waist and the small of your back. At first, your

Figure 6–50. You can also hang onto the mane or the saddle without letting go of the rein. Here the rider is sitting the trot. Her right hand is on the right rein and on Anrock's mane. Her left hand holds the left rein and keeps Anrock on the track. Notice that she is leaning too far forward for the sitting trot. Also, her heels should not be in Anrock's sides.

Figure 6–51a. Now the rider is sitting the trot again, but she has even worse form than before. You should never lean backward in the saddle.

Figure 6–51b. Your position while rising at the trot should be the same as your position rising at the walk. You will find it more difficult to stay up, so be sure to grab the mane or the saddle.

back will be stiff, and you will bounce in the saddle. You must limber your back until only your back moves at the trot. I know of only two exercises that help here, and one of them is simply hours in the saddle at the sitting trot. The other is the hula hoop.

SIMPLE TURNS

Turns using the leading rein are identical at all gaits. At the trot, don't turn too sharply. Keep your horse trotting around the turns.

C / The Rising Position at the Trot

The rising position, if done correctly, is the same at all gaits. Actually, practicing the rising position at the trot will be a little harder for you, and thus do you more good. You can even do simple turns while in this position, to vary your practice sessions. Hang onto the mane with one hand, if necessary (keep a rein in each hand), and lead your mount into a turn with the other. Practice both the rising position and the sitting position at the trot until you feel fairly comfortable. This might take you more than one practice session, depending upon your general physical condition.

LESSON 3:
POSTING AND THE QUICK DISMOUNT

Tack and mount.	
Review the sitting trot, with turns.	**10 minutes**
Review the rising position at the trot.	**10 minutes**
A / Post at a walk.	**5 minutes**
B / Post at the trot.	**25 minutes**
C / Quick dismount at the halt and the walk.	**10 minutes**

A / Posting at a Walk

THE PURPOSE OF POSTING

Posting was invented to smooth the roughness of the trot. When posting, you can ride the trot much faster and over much longer periods of time without fatigue. Posting accomplishes this by effectively diluting the bouncing action of the trot.

HOW TO POST AT THE WALK

You will post at the walk only during this lesson. The exercise is designed to introduce you to posting. Once you have the idea and have begun learning the form, you should begin practicing posting at a trot. To post at the walk, watch your horse's shoulder. Either shoulder will do; however, it is better to watch the shoulder that is closer to the rail, for reasons that will become apparent later. You should soon notice that the shoulder moves forward and backwards with the motion of the foreleg. When the foreleg is lifted off the ground, the shoulder moves forward. When the forefoot returns to the ground, the shoulder moves down, and then backward. Now, try to follow this motion with your seat. When the shoulder moves forward, rock forward with your pelvis and go into the rising position. When the shoulder comes back, settle down into the saddle, holding your body with a slight forward inclination. Your heels should stay down, and your legs should be still. Rise from your knees and thighs. Steady your hands against your horse's neck, if necessary. You should not pull yourself up with the reins, but you may pull up on the mane.

B / Posting at the Trot

HOW TO POST AT THE TROT

After a few minutes of practice at the walk, you should try to post the trot. The trot is easier to post, as the horse will toss you gently from the saddle with each rising beat. You may watch the same shoulder to cue you when to rise, or you may look ahead and try to follow the rhythm of your horse. Rise with one beat of his hooves—his action will help you. On the next beat, sit. As the trot is a two-beat gait, you will always rise with the beat of the same diagonal pair of legs. The rhythm is up-down, up-down, and so on.

POSITION AT THE POSTING TROT

You should lean slightly forward at all times. When you take the rising position, move forward and upward. To sit, move backward and down. Your upper body should remain at the same inclination at all times. Do not arch or hollow your back. Keep your head up. Use your knee and hip joints as springs, and keep your heels relaxed and slightly lowered. When done correctly, posting should seem effortless. Try to let the horse do all the work. You may hold on to the mane to steady your hands, if you desire. Do not pull yourself up with the reins.

C / The Quick Dismount

Sometimes you might want, or need, to get off your horse in a hurry. Perhaps he is running away and approaching an oncoming train. Maybe he's started bucking, and you are sure he'll toss

Figure 6–52. The rider is posting to the outside foreleg. She is out of the saddle when Anrock's outside foreleg is in the air. She is hanging on to the mane to steady herself. Some horses have a springier trot than others. Anrock's trot throws his rider high in the air. Some horses have almost no spring in their gaits. These animals make posting difficult, and you must post very close to the saddle.

Figure 6–53. The first and most important step in the quick dismount is to take both feet out of the stirrups. If you try to get off with a foot in a stirrup, you might get hung up and seriously injured.

you off. The quick dismount was designed for cases like these. You will have trouble getting up the nerve to bail out if you haven't practiced; therefore, you should do at least one emergency dismount per lesson. Start your experience at the halt, then work up until you are dismounting while your horse is cantering. In this lesson, you will dismount at the halt and at the walk. In the next lesson, you will slide off at the trot. You should wait many more lessons before you attempt to dismount from the canter. Always practice this skill on soft ground away from potentially dangerous obstructions.

To make a quick dismount, first drop (take your feet out of) both stirrups! Don't forget this step! Next, in the English saddle, lean forward and circle both hands around your horse's neck. Don't be shy: Give him a good hug. Now, bring your right leg behind you over the saddle and drop to the ground. In the Western saddle, place both your hands upon the pommel and swing

Figure 6–54. English riders should next embrace the horse and slide off to the left, Western riders must vault off in order to avoid the horn of the saddle. Place your left hand on the horse's neck, your right hand on the swells of the saddle, and swing off to the left.

your right leg behind you over the saddle. Vault to the ground a little way away from your mount. In both styles of riding, you should let go of the reins. And remember to practice only in an enclosed area—you don't want to lose your horse! Incidentally, don't be alarmed if your horse stops moving as soon as you begin to dismount. Get off anyway.

LESSON 4: DIAGONALS

Tack and mount.	
Review sitting trot, with turns.	**10 minutes**
Review rising position at the trot.	**10 minutes**
Review posting at the trot.	**10 minutes**
A / **Learn the correct diagonals.**	**10 minutes**
B / **Change diagonals.**	**10 minutes**

> **Practice turns at the posting trot, with**   **10 minutes**
> **diagonal changes when necessary.**
> **Quick dismount from the trot.**

A / Correct Diagonals

In Lesson 2 we discussed the mechanisms of the trot. You learned that the trot is a two-beat gait, and that each beat is produced by a pair of diagonal legs. The right foreleg and left hindleg is the right diagonal; the left foreleg and the right hindleg is the left diagonal. When you post, you should always post with the hindleg that is towards the center of a turn. This action gives the horse greater stability. Therefore, in a ring you should post with the *outside foreleg*. When you are moving around the ring clockwise, the rail will be to your left, and you should post with the horse's *left diagonal pair* of legs. This is called taking the left diagonal. When the rail is to your right, you should take the right diagonal (see Figure 6-55 for diagrams).

To take the left diagonal, for example, watch your mount's left shoulder. When the shoulder moves forward, you should rise; when it moves backwards, you should sit. Once you have learned to tell the diagonals apart—by studying and following the shoulders—you should begin posting without looking down. Try to guess which diagonal you are on by feel. Feel is a very important part of horsemanship. After you guess, glance down to see if you felt correctly. Remember also that you should always be on the diagonal by the rail of the ring, or the "outside diagonal." If you are not on the correct one, you should change. Once you develop your feel, you will be able to check and see if you are correct without looking, and change before anyone else knows you made a mistake.

B / Changing Diagonals

To change your diagonals, you need not stop posting and try again. You can change quickly and easily by sitting a single extra beat. Usually you post to the count of one-two, one-two.

Right diagonal

Change from
right to left
diagonals

Left diagonal

Figure 6–55. Posting the diagonals and changing diagonals.

On the count one, you rise; on the count two, you sit. To change diagonals, count one time like this: "One-two-three." On the count one, rise; on counts two and three, sit. Then it is time for count one again, and you rise—on the other diagonal.

You should practice changing diagonals until it becomes second nature to you (see Figure 6-55 for diagrams). In this lesson, practice both along the rails, and on simple turns through the middle of the ring. If you plan to change directions in a turn through the ring, you should change diagonals in the middle of the ring (see Figure 6-56).

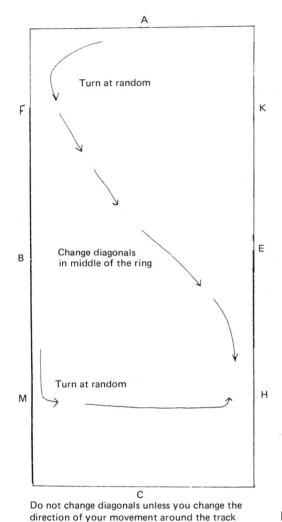

A

F

Turn at random

K

B

Change diagonals
in middle of the ring

E

M

Turn at random

H

C

Do not change diagonals unless you change the
direction of your movement around the track

Figure 6–56. Simple turns through the ring.

LESSON 4A:
THE CANTER FOR CASUAL RIDERS

Do *not* take this lesson if you plan to advance to the lessons in Chapter 7. This lesson is for casual riders, those who wish to ride only occasionally.

Mount.

Review the sitting trot.   **10 minutes**

Review the rising position at the trot.	**10 minutes**
Review diagonals at the trot.	**10 minutes**
A / **Elementary cantering.**	**30 minutes**
Quick dismount from the trot.	

A / Elementary Cantering

A canter is a slow, controlled gallop. It is a three-beat gait that gives a rocking motion to the rider. As the canter is faster than the walk or trot, and has both up-and-down and back-and-forth motion, it is the most difficult of the gaits to learn. Many people ride the canter without falling off the horse; however, only a small percentage of riders are able to canter with control and form. If you wish to canter correctly, go on to Lesson 5. By Lesson 11, when the canter is again introduced, you will be able to learn a correct seat. If you wish merely to ride fast and stay on, follow these steps:

1. Trot your horse. You may sit or take the rising position. Hang on to the mane or the saddle.

2. Kick with your heels. Do not take your knees off the saddle! Some horses will respond to the spoken word, "Canter!"

3. Your horse will probably go into a very fast trot. Hang on and keep kicking. Sooner or later he will canter.

4. When he begins to canter, stop kicking. Hang on. You will probably be most comfortable if you ride in the rising position.

5. Do not pull on your horse's mouth, unless you wish to return to a trot. Then give a light, steady pull until he begins to trot. He will go into a fast trot. Be prepared.

6. Keep him cantering by kicking with both heels should he slow to a trot.

7. Do not canter in any enclosure smaller than the riding ring. It is too hard on your horse's legs to run around in small circles.

8. Do not canter in open fields. He might run away.

9. Remember at all times that this is a very crude way to canter. Your method of taking the canter is rough and hard on you and on your horse. Your seat in the saddle is very insecure: If your horse does anything unexpected, you will probably fall. For best results, skip this lesson and take the time to learn to canter correctly.

TEST YOUR FORM: WESTERN

For best results, have a friend snap several pictures of you while you ride. Compare the pictures with the drawing in Figure 6-26 and answer the questions below:

1. Are you sitting straight in the saddle?
2. Are your toes even with or slightly to the front of your knees?
3. Are your heels lower than your toes?
4. Are you close to the saddle at all times?
5. Are your eyes up and your shoulders back?
6. Do you look comfortable and relaxed?

TEST YOUR FORM: ENGLISH

For best results, have a friend snap several pictures of you while you ride. Compare the pictures with the drawing in Figure 6-25 and answer the questions below:

1. Are your hands over, and slightly in front of, your horse's withers?
2. Is your body vertical, except when posting? Is your back straight?
3. Are your heels down at all times? Do your toes turn at a relaxed angle?
4. Is there a straight line from your knee through your toes?
5. Are your eyes up and your shoulders back?
6. Do you look comfortable and relaxed?

TEST: PART III, CHAPTER 6, LESSONS 1–4A

Written Tests (100 points possible; passing grade, 75)

1. Define the following terms completely (50 points, 5 points each):
   a. Correct position at the walk
   b. Mechanics of the walk
   c. The leading rein
   d. The rising position
   e. Mechanics of the trot
   f. Correct position at sitting trot
   g. Purpose of posting
   h. Position at the posting trot
   i. Quick dismount
   j. The left diagonal

2. True or false (50 points, 2 points each):
   a. Stand on the off side and lay the pad gently on your horse's back when you saddle.
   b. Always check the off side of the saddle before you tighten the girth or cinch.
   c. To bridle, hold the crown of the bridle in your right hand, the bit in your left.
   d. If your horse refuses to open his mouth for the bit, rub a little sugar on it.
   e. The strap of the dropped noseband should fall about an inch below your mount's jawbone.
   f. The bit should fit loosely against your horse's lips. It is better if it is too loose than too tight.
   g. The first step in mounting is to tighten the girth.

h. Mounting from the front is designed for use in Western saddles.

i. Always grip your reins with your fingers tightly closed.

j. In an English saddle, the deepest point should be in the exact center.

k. When sitting in the saddle, keep your knees as close to the saddle as you can.

l. The walk is a three-beat gait.

m. Never talk while you ride. You will confuse your horse.

n. To make your horse stop, draw the reins backwards until they tighten against his mouth.

o. To use the leading rein, merely pull your hand out a few inches from its normal position, and lead the horse into the turn.

p. Your position at the walk is different from your position at the halt in that you lean slightly forward.

q. The rising position is an excellent exercise for developing correct leg position.

r. Correct form in dismounting is very important.

s. The first few times you trot you should grab the mane or the pommel of the saddle.

t. The sitting trot is not very important in building your riding skills.

u. At the sitting trot, always lean slightly forward.

v. Posting was invented to smooth the roughness of the trot.

w. When you post, you should hollow your back.

x. The quick dismount was designed to get you off your horse in a hurry.

y. To post the right diagonal, rise from the saddle when the left shoulder goes forward.

Riding Tests (Passing grade, 8 out of 10)

Before you go on to Chapter 7, you should be able to do each of the following:

1. Tack up by yourself.
2. Mount by yourself.
3. Quick dismount from a trot.
4. Do a simple turn at the sitting trot.
5. Halt from a walk.
6. Sit the trot for three minutes without hanging on with your hands.
7. Stay in the rising position for one minute at the trot without holding on with your hands.
8. Post for five minutes in rhythm.
9. Do four changes of diagonal without a mistake.
10. Ride in the correct position at the sitting trot:
    a. heels down
    b. back supple
    c. shoulders square
    d. back straight
    e. head up
    f. elbows at your side, hands still.

7 Basic Riding Skills

This chapter, covering Lessons 5 through 16, includes everything you need to know to complete your basic riding knowledge. After learning this material you should be able to show, pleasure ride, compete in elementary dressage tests (a form of English horsemanship where the horse is judged on his performance), jump over obstacles, ride in Western games, and then—if you desire—go on to advanced work.

Each lesson is designed to introduce one or more new skills. Unless you have previous riding experience, or are extremely talented, you will not be able to master the new skills in the one hour allowed. Therefore, you should plan several practice sessions to go along with each lesson. I am including Practice Rides, and other drills that you may use while you build your riding skills. You should plan to practice each lesson for at least three hours. Many lessons will take literally dozens of hours for complete mastery: Experts estimate that it takes hundreds of hours to become an accomplished rider. However, you need not practice the lessons beyond the time it takes you to develop minimal competence. Each lesson reviews all previous lessons, and you will never actually stop practicing any particular skill. After each group of four lessons are tests which will help you judge your progress. Until you can pass the tests, you should not go on to the next group of four lessons.

You will notice that the lessons in this chapter cover what we call "school figures." School figures are movements you will ride in the ring—for example, circles. These movements are part of basic dressage. If you learn them as they are described in the lessons, you will be able to ride elementary dressage tests. I have included these figures because dressage is becoming a very popular form of competition; however, you should learn the school figures even if you never enter a dressage arena. As the name implies, school figures are an excellent way to learn riding skills.

Also in these lessons are drills using bending poles and cavaletti. You can learn to ride without practicing these drills. However, the drills are excellent for teaching you control of your mount. They also provide variety, making your practice sessions more interesting.

Jumping is discussed for huntseat riders only! Do not try to jump unless you have a jumping saddle and a hard hat. Jumping is a valuable skill that many riders enjoy. But do not jump unless you desire to learn: You need not jump to become a good rider.

At the end of this Chapter are your final exams. Until you pass them, you have not really mastered your basic riding skills. Remember that you must practice many hours to become a competent rider. Don't rush yourself or become discouraged, and you will eventually be able to ride with skill and grace.

LESSON 5:
NO STIRRUPS, NO HANDS

	Mount.	
	Review posting and changing diagonals.	**10 minutes**
	Review simple turns and the sitting trot.	**5 minutes**
A /	**Ride the sitting trot without stirrups.**	**10 minutes**
B /	**Ride the posting trot without holding on.**	**35 minutes**
	Quick dismount from the trot.	

A / Sitting at the Trot without Stirrups

This exercise is excellent for teaching you to ride down in the saddle, and for strengthening your seat. First (in an English saddle) you should take the stirrups and leathers off your saddle, or cross them over your horse's withers. Then, let your legs hang in a relaxed, natural position. Do not try to push your heels down, or to hold your legs as if you had stirrups. Your toes should be lower than your heels. When you trot, hold your shoulders square and relax your back. Do not draw your heels up into your mount. If you feel you must hang on, grab the horse's mane or the pommel of your saddle.

B / Posting at the Trot without Hanging On

Since trained riders rarely hang on, you should begin to practice all your lessons without a hand on the horse's mane or the pommel. Posting is rather difficult to do with good hands and takes a special effort on your part. When your horse trots, his head remains absolutely still. (Remember, at the walk, he nods his head, and you should move your hands.) To stay with your horse's mouth at the trot, you must hold your hands absolutely still. Since you are posting, and moving your body up and down,

Figure 7–1. When you sit the trot without stirrups in an English saddle, you can cross the stirrups on your horse's neck, out of the way. In a Western saddle, you simply kick your feet out of the stirrups. You should ride with your toes down and your ankles relaxed. Don't try to hold your legs as if you had stirrups—doing this would stiffen your whole body. The rider is in excellent form except that her toes should not be so far out. She has Chocolate on contact. At this stage in your lessons, you should let the reins go loose and hang on to the saddle or the mane.

your hands will tend to move up and down. This is a very bad habit, although everyone does it at first. There are several tricks you can use *temporarily* to help you hold your hands in one place. These tricks are as follows:

1. Grab a little mane in both hands and hang on.

2. Drop the reins for a few strides and post with your hands on your hips.

3. Put the thumb of each hand on your horse's neck and keep them there.

4. Post with a small glass of water in your hand.

While Western riders are not required to post, they might do this exercise as it is excellent for developing quiet hands—that is, hands which do not pull on the reins and interfere with your horse's mouth.

I am now going to describe a few more exercises you can use in your practice sessions to add variety, and to help build your riding skills. They are:

1. Rotate your neck. Slowly turn your head from right to left.

2. Rotate your arms. Take each arm, one at a time, and make large, slow circles through the air.

3. Stroke your horse on the right shoulder with your right hand.

4. Stroke your horse on the left shoulder with your right hand.

5. Rotate your feet slowly.

The above exercises should be done while riding the walk, sitting trot, posting trot, and the rising position. Do them only in the ring under quiet conditions.

LESSON 6:
RIDING BAREBACK (OPTIONAL)

A / **Mount bareback.**	**5 minutes**
B / **Walk and do simple turns.**	**10 minutes**
C / **Rising position at the walk.**	**10 minutes**

D / **Sitting the trot.**	**10 minutes**
E / **Rising position at the trot.**	**10 minutes**
F / **Posting at the walk and trot.**	**15 minutes**
Dismount.	

A / Mount Bareback

Several ways to mount bareback exist. According to theory, you should be able to vault onto your mount's back. Actually, I always look for a log or the back of a car to climb onto so I can simply slide into place. For this lesson, you may mount from a block, or have someone boost you aboard, or you may try vaulting.

There are two ways to vault onto a horse. In the first, slightly safer method, you should stand by your mount's shoulder. Grab the reins and the mane in your left hand. Then, on the count of three, give a tremendous jump, fling your right leg high in the air, and try to toss your right arm and right leg over the top of your horse. If you get them far enough over, you will be able to scramble on aboard. Needless to say, the taller you are the easier this method will be.

The second method is not as safe: You probably shouldn't try it unless you have someone to hold your mount. Otherwise, he may turn and kick you, or shy and run away. To begin, stand six feet away from your mount's left side. Take three or four running steps, grab your horse's mane and back, and jump upwards as high as you can. The object is to land on your belly on top of him. Once up there, you can swing around into the sitting position.

As I said, I always mount from a block, or climb up a gate, or something. However, you might be more athletic than I.

B / Walk and Simple Turns

Riding bareback has several advantages. The one I like is the simplicity of it. You need no saddle and therefore no special riding clothes, you may wear any type of clothing. I frequently

Figure 7–2. Chocolate is wearing a curb bit (actually, a three-in-one pelham) for better control. You might want to put your horse in a mild curb or a hackamore when you practice bareback riding.

ride bareback in shorts and sneakers. It's a good idea to wear a helmet, in case you lose your seat. Also, if your mount is fat and round, bareback is very comfortable. It is excellent for building nerve and balance in a rider.

However, I do not recommend that you ride bareback too often at this point. A few practice sessions should be enough. Bareback riding does not develop leg position and tends to deteriorate general riding form.

Sit behind your horse's withers—far enough back so that you do not hurt yourself. Stretch your legs down and sit on the points of your buttocks and your crotch, as in riding with a saddle. Let your lower legs hang relaxed.

When your mount walks, you should be able to feel the movement in his back. Go with it, relaxing your lower back. Simple turns are the same bareback as with a saddle.

C / Rising Position at the Walk

This exercise is not impossible, if you have developed muscles in your thighs. Keeping your lower legs relaxed, rock forward on

Figure 7–3. Don't worry too much about your legs when you ride bareback. Just sit up straight, push your buttocks out behind you, and try to relax. If you stiffen your legs, you'll probably fall off. Keep your mount on a loose rein and hang on to the mane. If your horse doesn't have a mane, you can tie a leather strap around his neck to serve as a handle.

Figure 7–4. To take the rising position bareback, grab hold of the mane and rise up on your thighs. This exercise will be very difficult, or even impossible, for you at first. Don't try to stay for more than a minute or so at a time. Be sure you keep your back straight and your heels out of your horse's sides.

137

your thighs until your seat is off your horse. Keep your back straight, with only a slight hollow in your lower back. You may brace on the mane if you must.

D / Sitting at the Trot

Put your horse into a slow trot and relax. If you feel yourself losing your seat, walk and start over. Sitting the trot bareback is excellent for developing relaxation in your back and legs. You should practice until it becomes easy for you. Remember to sit up straight, let your lower back be limber, and relax your legs. Don't let your legs come up or go back into your horse's side. Don't allow yourself to slide back so that you are bouncing along on your rear. You must always try to maintain the correct position. You may grab the mane if you feel more comfortable hanging onto something.

Figure 7–5. The secret of sitting the trot bareback is this: Relax! Grab the mane and hold yourself down until you are able to sit without bouncing. Be careful not to pull your heels up or start holding on with the reins.

E / Rising Position at the Trot

You will find this very difficult to do correctly. Practice for only a few minutes at a time, sitting the trot or walking between times.

F / Posting Bareback

Posting is not difficult if you let the horse do the work. Practice a little at the walk to get the feel, then start at the trot. Don't try to rise very far off your horse. Keep your lower legs relaxed. You should lean slightly forward and let your horse rock you forward and backwards. After you get the hang of it, practice the diagonals and changing diagonals. If you slide out of position, walk and start over.

LESSON 7:
USING THE CROP AND THE REINS

Mount.

Review the sitting trot, with and without stirrups.   15 minutes

Review the posting trot without holding on. Change diagonals and work on developing feel.   15 minutes

A / Use of the crop.

B / Holding the reins Western style (Western).

C / Neck reining.

D / Riding on contact (English).

Practice the above four exercises at the walk, sitting trot, posting trot (Western   30 minutes

Figure 7–6. When you carry a crop, hold it across your horse's withers so he can't see it unless you bring it down to use it.

riders need not post), and in the rising position.

Quick dismount from the trot.

A / Using the Crop

Your horse may or may not require the use of a crop. A crop is a short whip, 18-28 inches long, carried by the rider as an aid in controlling the horse. If you don't own a crop, you may cut a short switch from a tree. If your animal is slow in responding to your heels, you might consider using a crop from the first lesson on. Even if he responds beautifully, you should practice carrying a crop during this lesson in order to familiarize yourself with the procedure.

While you mount, you may slip the crop under the saddle, or into your boot, or you may hold it in your left hand along with the reins. Do not hold it in your right hand and wave it around as you climb aboard: You may frighten, or accidentally strike, your mount. Once you are up and ready to go, take the crop in your hand. Use the hand that is by the rail of the ring, so that the crop will act upon the outside of the horse on the turns. For example, if you turn your horse to the left, you should hold the crop in your right hand. You must hold both the rein and the crop if you ride English. Western riders will be riding with one hand on the reins beginning this lesson: They may hold the reins in one hand, and the crop in the other.

Take the crop by the handle. Do not wrap the loop around your hand or hang it over your wrist. The loop is designed for hanging the crop from a nail in the tack room. If placed around your hand it can be dangerous—you may catch the crop on something and cut your hand badly.

The crop should be held pointing upwards across the horse's withers. If held this way, the crop is invisible to the horse. Since some horses become very nervous when they see a crop, keeping it invisible is a good idea. Also, held in this position, the crop is ready for instant use.

When you are ready to use your crop (say that for some reason your mount did not respond to your leg), slip both reins into your other hand. Then bring your hand down so that your horse can see the crop. This may produce the desired results. If not, continue to lower your hand swiftly, and pop the horse behind your ankle. Do not hit him on the flank (too severe) or the rump (too mild). Then, immediately raise your hand to the withers and take the rein.

Until you learn how your horse responds, be cautious in the use of the crop. Some animals may jump forward at the slightest touch. Many horses, however, respond only to a good pop. Always show him the crop first. If that doesn't work, try a light touch. Then, if he fails to respond, give him a firm, but not hard, pop with the crop. In general, crops are used to improve your mount's response to your leg. You may use them to make your horse move forward, or to make him turn.

B / Holding the Reins Western-Style

Trained Western riders usually ride with the reins in one hand. It is now time for you to begin practicing this skill.

You may use either hand as the rein hand. In horse shows

Figure 7–7. To hold the reins Western style, first make sure both reins are the same length. Then put them together and grab them so that your thumb points toward your horse's head. Your wrist should be relaxed. You may use either hand on the reins. Your other hand should be placed on your knee or across your chest. You may hold on to the saddle horn if you want to do so in these lessons.

they require that you use only one hand, and that you do not change the reins from one hand to the other during a class. However, during these lessons you may switch the reins as often as you wish. You will find it necessary to switch from one hand to the other if you must use a crop.

First of all, make sure you have a Western bit on your horse. In Chapter 1 you rode with an English snaffle, in order to develop your skills without the abuse of the severe Western bit. Now, you should have enough experience to be able to use a Western bit without abusing your horse. You will need a Western bit for full control if you ride with one hand in the style here discussed.

When you take the reins, make sure they are of equal length from your hand to the bit. You should have a little slack. Take the reins in one hand so that they enter between your thumb and forefinger, and leave between your little finger and your palm. Your hand must be bent forward so that your thumb points towards the horse's head. From now on, when you want to stop or slow your speed, you will raise your hand in a series of slight jerks until your mount responds (see Figure 7-9). You must never pull on the reins while using a Western bit. This bit

Figure 7–8. Hold your rein hand in front of the saddle and let the reins be a little loose. If you aren't careful, your body will twist at the shoulders. Here, the rider is carrying her right shoulder ahead of her left shoulder. You should try to keep your shoulders even. Chocolate is working in a three-in-one pelham rather than a real Western bit. The reins are attached to the curb rings of the bit so that the pelham is acting like a Western curb in her mouth.

Figure 7–9. Hand motions in stopping.

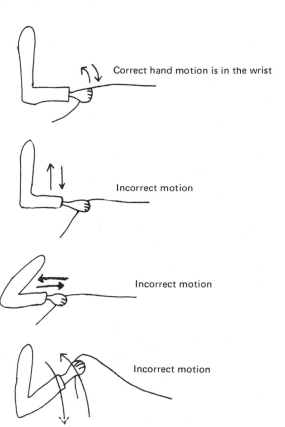

Correct hand motion is in the wrist

Incorrect motion

Incorrect motion

Incorrect motion

is very severe: A light touch should give you all the control you need. Watch your horse's mouth. If he opens his mouth, you are using your hand too heavily.

To turn, you must learn to use the neck rein.

C / Neck Reining

Any horse can be trained to neck rein: however, western horses are trained to respond almost exclusively to this form of control. Neck reining is very valuable when the rider uses only one hand on the reins. A horse which "reins good" will react to the lightest touch of the rein upon his neck. The neck rein is sometimes called the "bearing rein." This is the only method of turning in which it is correct for the horse to look away from the direction of the turn.

The rein acts upon the animal's neck and shoulders, causing him to shift his weight to the rear and move away from the rein (see Figures 7-10 and 7-11).

To neck rein (for example, to the left), pull your rein across your horse's neck by moving your rein hand to the left about ten inches. Your hand must move on a horizontal plane: Do not pull your hand up or down. The right rein should act upon your mount's neck while the left rein remains slack. At the same time, you should use your seat and legs as aids to help the horse turn correctly.

Up to this point, I have not mentioned the use of the seat and legs in control. I think you must develop some balance and coordination before you can use these aids correctly. However, your seat and legs are actually far more important than your hands in managing your horse.

During the neck rein to the left, you should tighten your left leg in a line over the cinch of the saddle. This is called "using your leg on the girth." Your right leg should tap your horse directly behind the cinch—called "using your leg behind the girth." Don't move your right leg more than six inches behind the cinch, and don't pull your calf up into your horse's belly (see Figure 7-13). If your horse fails to respond to your heel, you may

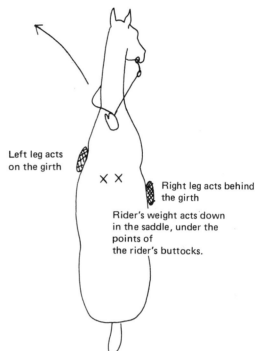

Left leg acts on the girth

Right leg acts behind the girth

Rider's weight acts down in the saddle, under the points of the rider's buttocks.

Figure 7–10. When you neck rein, you should draw your hand straight over, so that the rein presses against the middle portion of your horse's neck. Don't pull your hand up or down. The rider is using the right neck rein to move Chocolate to the left. The left rein is loose and has no action. The right rein is pushing Chocolate to the left.

Figure 7–11. Neck rein.

use the crop on the right behind your heel. Always, however, try the heel first. Sooner or later he will begin to respond, and you will no longer need the crop.

As you apply your heels, you should use your seat aid. Press down with your seat so that the points of your buttocks (the two little bones in your buttocks) are heavy against the saddle. Do this by stiffening your back. Do not lean backwards from your shoulders. Also, do not lean forward, or to either side, and do not push your weight into either stirrup. Keep your seat balanced in the saddle at all times.

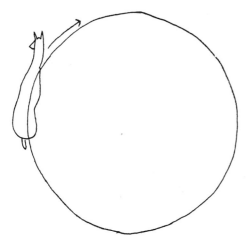 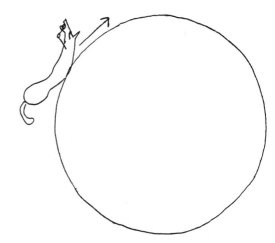

Figure 7–12a. A correct turn with the neck rein. The haunches follow the shoulders. The horse looks away from the direction of movement.

Figure 7–12b. An incorrect turn with the neck rein. The horse skids with his haunches. His head is raised and his mouth is open because of pulling by the rider.

Figure 7–13. Leg action: (a) behind the girth; (b) on the girth; (c) in front of the girth.

The sequence of the turn should be as follows (see Figure 7-12a and b):

1. Decide where you will turn.
2. Press the points of your buttocks into the saddle.
3. Apply the neck rein and your legs at the same time!
4. Use the crop if necessary.

D / Riding on Contact

English riders may or may not practice neck reining (it is a valuable skill) but they should start learning to ride on contact. When you are in contact with your horse, you have better, more subtle, control. You are able to get a more polished performance. However, unless your hands are quiet (do not jerk around outside your control) and soft (don't pull upon his mouth) you may cause your mount a lot of pain. Remember that the reins are connected directly to his mouth by way of the bit. A horse's mouth should be very sensitive, and will be—if not abused by poor hands.

To ride on contact—something you will never learn if you don't practice—shorten your reins until there is a straight line from your horse's mouth to your elbows. Your wrists should be straight, but relaxed. Your fingers should close around the reins loosely. Grip the reins firmly only with your thumb and forefinger. The other fingers should act only when you need to use the reins for direction or control.

At the walk, your horse will nod his head. To remain in constant, non-jerking contact with his mouth, you must move your hands in rhythm with his head. When his head goes down, you must allow your hands to go forward and down; when his head comes up, your hands should come backwards and up. Remember, your aim is to keep the same contact with the mouth of your horse at all times. The feel on the reins should always be the same. You must relax your arms and shoulders, and use your hands and reins like fine lines of communication going from your brain to your horse (see Figures 7-15a—16b).

Figure 7–14. The rider has Anrock on contact at the walk. There is a straight line from the bit to her elbows. Anrock is moving with an extended head and neck. You shouldn't pull your horse's head up when you put him on contact. Your feel on the reins should be very light. The rider certainly shouldn't have her left toe turned outward.

Figure 7–15a. Good hands are relaxed and do not pull. They are quiet hands; they remain steady and do not jerk. The wrist is straight. The whole hand is turned at an angle of about 45 degrees to the horse.
Figure 7–15b. Poor hands grip the reins. The wrist is bent and tense.
Figure 7–15c. Pulling hands are the worst hands. The wrist bends inward and locks. These hands pull against the horse's mouth.

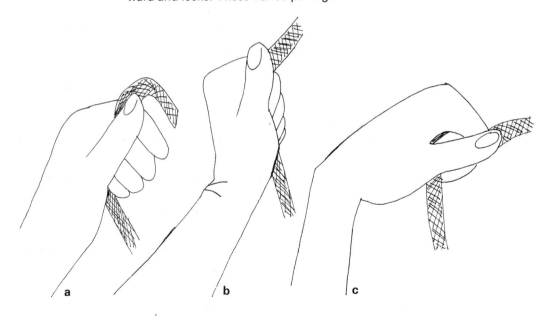

a   b   c

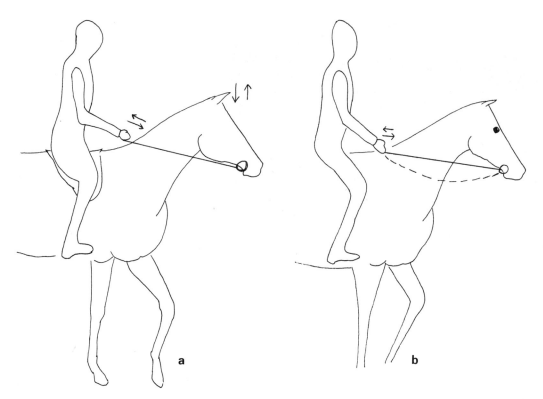

Figure 7–16a. The horse nods its head as it walks. Good hands will follow this action and keep a steady contact with the horse's mouth.
Figure 7–16b. Poor hands are not on good contact with the horse's mouth. They move very little, so that the reins pull tight when the horse lowers his head and loosen when he raises his head. As a result, the horse is jerked in the mouth with each stride.

At the trot, your horse will hold his head still. Therefore, you must hold your hands still. If you have learned to post with quiet hands, this will be fairly easy for you. Learning to follow the horse's mouth at the walk and the canter will give you more difficulty. Watch his mouth while you ride the sitting trot on contact. If you are using your hands correctly, you will see that your horse is relaxed in the mouth. His jaw will look relaxed, and his mouth will be passive or he will be slightly chewing the bit. If you are abusing his mouth with heavy or jerking hands, your horse will close his mouth like a steel trap, and pull. He

Figure 7–17. Sitting the trot on contact, the rider holds her hands still. Neither your horse's head nor your hands should move at the trot.

might also open his mouth wide, or toss his head about, or bend his neck so that his chin is behind the vertical—that is, behind the bit.

Practice riding on contact at the walk, the sitting trot, and the posting trot. Unless you can ride the rising position at the trot with both hands on your hips, you should not try to ride on

Figure 7–18. The rider is posting to the left diagonal, on contact. Unfortunately, her hands and her heels have come up out of position. These are common faults at the posting trot. She should also be leaning a little forward.

Figure 7–19. Posting with the right diagonal, the rider has started pulling herself up on the reins. You can see that she is leaning backward and is pulling on the bit. She should be leaning forward, with her hands much lower.

contact at this time. Every so often, give your mount a rest. Let him walk around the ring completely relaxed on a really loose rein. When you put him back on contact, do so at the walk or trot, never at the halt.

Figure 7–20. Quiet hands remain steady at the trot. Poor hands jerk up and down as the rider posts.

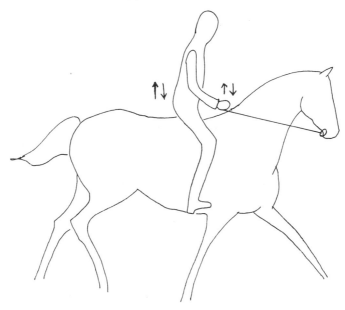

LESSON 8:
GUIDING WITH THE REINS; SCHOOL FIGURES I

Mount.

Review holding the reins (Western).

Review riding on contact (English).   **10 minutes**

Review neck reining.

A / The direct rein. The indirect rein (English).

B / The circle and the diagonal   **30 minutes**

C / Bending poles.   **20 minutes**

Dismount. Start practicing the correct dismount.

A / Direct Rein and Indirect Rein

DIRECT REIN

The direct rein effect is used in both stopping and turning your horse. It is much more effective than the methods described earlier. First, I will discuss using the direct rein to turn. In a later lesson, I will tell you how to use this rein effect to stop your mount. Until then, you should continue to stop as I described in Chapter 1.

To get full use from the direct rein, you should have your horse on contact. To turn (for example, to the right) bring your right hand about an inch to the right. Then draw it about an inch to the rear, or farther if your horse fails to respond. As soon as your mount reacts to the rein, fix your hand, and hold it steady until he completes the turn. Your horse should turn his head to the right so that you can see the bones around his right eye. He should not turn his head away from the action of the direct rein (see Figure 7-21). Nor should he turn his head too far to the right. Properly, the direct rein is used in combination with the indirect rein, the legs, and the seat.

INDIRECT REIN

To use the indirect rein effect in a turn to the right, bring your left hand slightly to the right, until the left rein is pressing against your horse's neck (see Figure 7-22). Do not raise or lower your hand from its normal position above the withers. Do not cross your hand to the right of the mid-line of the withers. This rein effect tends to push your horse's shoulders to the right. When used with the right direct rein, it keeps him from overbending his neck to the right.

Figure 7–21. The right direct rein. **Figure 7–22.** The left indirect rein.

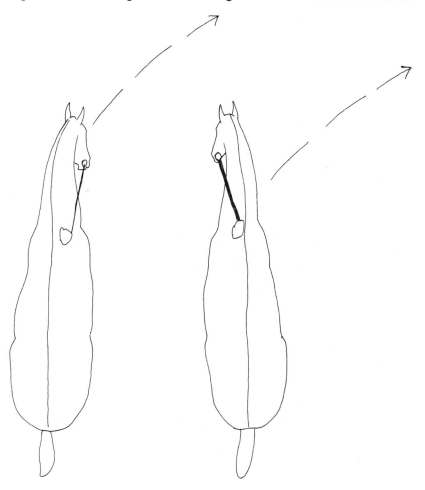

DIRECT AND INDIRECT REIN USED TOGETHER

Actually, you should use both the rein effects to turn. Each complements the other. Used together, they make for a smooth, even turn (see Figure 7-24). The sharpness of the turn will be determined by the degree of movement of your hands, and by the action of your legs and seat.

Figure 7–23. Anrock is trotting to the left for the direct and indirect reins. Notice that the right rein is against his neck and that the rider's right heel is active behind the girth. Anrock is turning rather sharply, yet his head and neck are in a line with his body. He is not skidding, as his hind feet are following the track of his fore feet. The rider is pressing her seat into the saddle to help push Anrock into the turn smoothly. She is carrying a long dressage whip, something you shouldn't carry until you develop a good seat and steady hands.

Figure 7–24. The right direct rein and the left indirect rein.

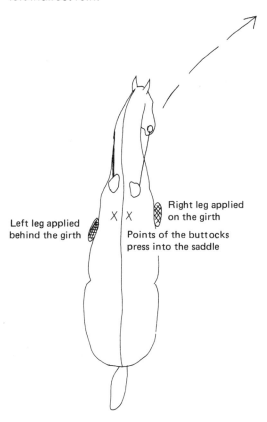

Left leg applied
behind the girth

Right leg applied
on the girth

Points of the buttocks
press into the saddle

A split second before you move your hands for the turn, you should prepare your mount by pressing the points of your buttocks (the two little bones in your buttocks) into the saddle. Do not, however, draw your knees up or lean backwards. Then, apply both the right direct and left indirect reins to put him into a right turn. At the same time, tighten your right leg from thigh to mid-calf over the girth of the saddle. Move your left leg no more than six inches behind the girth, and tap with your heel. Keep your weight pushed into the saddle. Do not lean either right or left. Keep your seat balanced over the center of the saddle, and your heels lower than your toes.

Remember, your hands should direct, or guide, your horse around the turn. Your legs and seat drive and make for a smooth, correct turn. Do not haul him around by your hands. Your mount should be relaxed and move freely without speeding or slowing his gait. He should turn his head only slightly in the direction of movement, and should not toss his head or open his mouth. It will probably take you a while to coordinate your arms and legs so that you get a perfect turn. The exercises in the next section will help you in your practice.

B / The Circle and the Diagonal

These two exercises are the first of a series of school figures that should be practiced by both English and Western riders. They will help you improve your riding skills, and add variety to your practice sessions (see Figure 7-25).

THE CIRCLE

A circle is a round figure the diameter, or width, of the ring. The letters you have painted on plywood and placed about your ring will help you to make circles and other schooling figures. You should always begin all schooling figures at the letters, to avoid confusing yourself and your horse. Using the letters will help both you and your horse keep the figures straight in your

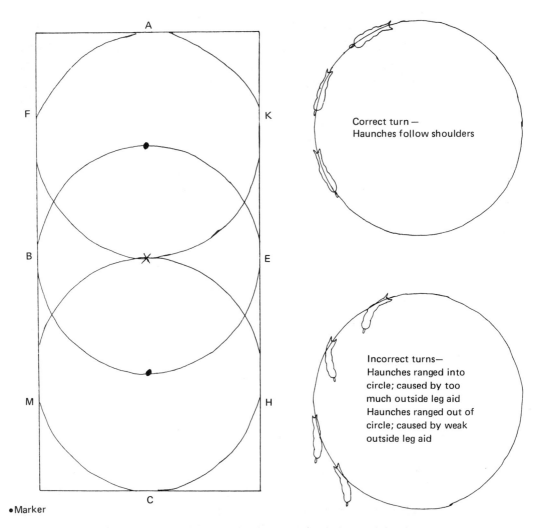

•Marker

Figure 7–25. Circles: the ring illustrated is 20 meters by 40 meters. The scale of the circles will hold true in any ring twice as long as it is wide.

Correct turn —
Haunches follow shoulders

Incorrect turns—
Haunches ranged into circle; caused by too much outside leg aid
Haunches ranged out of circle; caused by weak outside leg aid

Figure 7–26. Correct and incorrect circles.

minds. You may circle at letters $A,C,B,$ or E. You will find making an absolutely round circle (although ideally, it should be absolutely round) very difficult. This problem is caused by the inability of most people to visualize the circle in their minds.

To make circling easier, you can use several tricks. The simplest is to mark the X. Place an object (block or board painted with an X) in the center of the ring—you should meas-ure to be sure you have placed the X correctly. Then, practice riding circles at letters E and B. Keep your eyes on the X, and try to stay equidistant from it at all times.

You may find that you must mark the circumference of the circle as well. Put small markers as indicated in Figure 7-25 or outline the circle with agricultural lime. Once you learn to ride a circle, you will not need these aids, as your eye will measure the circle for you. However, do not hesitate to use markers as long as you feel they are necessary. For correct and incorrect circles, see Figure 7-26.

THE DIAGONAL

A diagonal in the ring is from letter H to letter F, or F to H; M to K, or K to M. Begin the figure when your knee is beside the first letter, and ride so that your knee will be beside the second letter when you enter the track. Between the two, you should ride an absolutely straight line. Keep your eyes on the second letter, and apply pressure with your upper calves so that your mount will neither hesitate nor waver from side to side. Notice that when you ride the diagonal, you change your direction of movement in the ring. Therefore, you should change posting diagonals at X (see Figures 7-27 and 7-30).

Do not allow your horse to speed up or slow down when you ride the diagonal. Make him move into the corner of the ring after you re-enter the track. From now on you should try to ride into all the corners of the ring: You should ride square cor-ners. You should not allow your mount to cut the corners.

C / Bending Poles

Bending poles are used as an aid in teaching turns, and as a means of adding variety to your lessons. Set the poles as indi-cated in Pole Bending I or II (you may use jump standards as bending poles). Practice bending around the poles as shown in

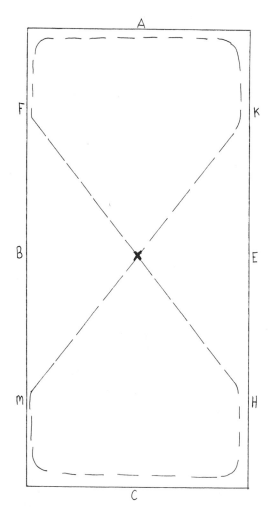

Figure 7–27. Diagonals.

Figure 7–28. The rider is using jump standards as bending poles. You may bend poles English or Western style and at the walk or the trot.

Figures 7-31 and 7-32. Do not try to turn too close to the poles. You don't want to hit them.

You may bend the poles at the walk, at the sitting or posting trot, or in the rising position. When you bend at the posting trot, you must change diagonals every time you change direction: You should always post the outside diagonal. Western riders should turn with the neck rein; English riders may use either the neck rein or the direct and indirect reins.

Figure 7–29. Chocolate is going around the pole, turning to the left leading rein. You should try to get close to the poles but not so close that you might knock one down.

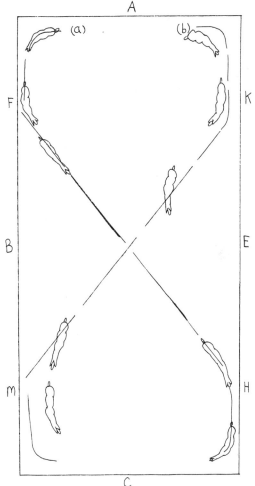

Figure 7–30. Correct and incorrect diagonals: (a) correct diagonal—the horse bends through the corners and travels a straight line from *F* to *H;* (b) incorrect diagonal—the horse cuts corners, skids on the turns, and wavers on the line from *K* to *M*.

Watch your horse to see that he does a smooth, relaxed turn with a relaxed head carriage and a soft jaw—not tense, or with an open mouth. If your horse grows harried or excited, relax your hands and use your legs and seat to a greater extent.

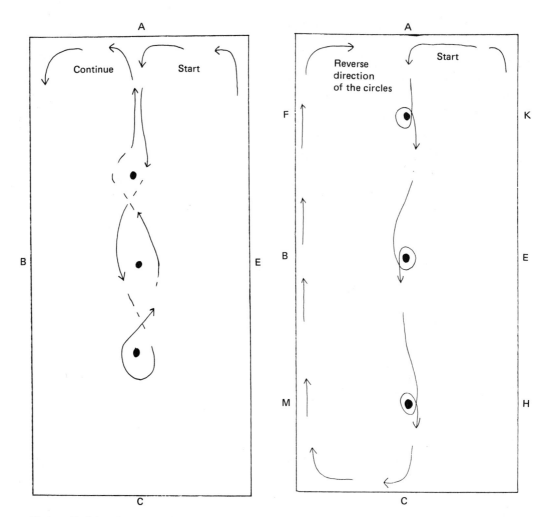

Figure 7–31. Pole bending I.

Figure 7–32. Pole bending II.

PRACTICE RIDE 1

The letters refer to letters in the ring (see Figure 7-25). You should always continue a movement from one letter to the next along the track. Begin the next movement when your shoulder is beside the letter indicated.

Letter	Movement
A	Begin at a walk. English riders should be on contact. Go to the right on the track.
B	Circle the width of the ring.
B	After the circle, continue at the walk.
C	Begin a posting trot (Western riders sit).
E	Circle the width of the ring.
E	After the circle, continue at the trot.
F–X–H	Ride the diagonal. English riders change posting diagonals at X.
C	Sit the trot.
M–X–K	Ride the diagonal.
F	Walk on a loose rein.
B	Take the rising position at the walk. Go all the way around the ring back to B.
B	Trot in the rising position once around the ring. Return to B.
B	Walk on loose rein.
C	Halt.

PRACTICE RIDE 2

Letter	Movement
A	Begin at the walk. English riders should be on contact. Go to the left on the track.

E	Begin the sitting trot.
C	Circle the width of the ring.
C	Sit the trot on the track to K.
K–X–M	Ride the diagonal.
C	English riders begin posting.
H–X–F	Ride the diagonal. (English riders change posting diagonals at X.)
E	Trot posting to E. Sit the trot at E.
C	Walk (English riders remain on contact).
B	Halt. Then continue on a loose rein.
F	Take the rising position at the walk. Go once around the ring back to F.
F	Trot in the rising position.
C	Sit the trot.
B	Walk.
A	Halt.

TEST YOUR FORM: WESTERN

For best results, have a friend snap several pictures of you while you ride. Compare the pictures with the drawing in Figure 6-25 and answer the questions below:

1. Are your arms in a straight line with your body?
2. Are you sitting straight in the saddle?
3. Are your toes even with, or just slightly in front of, your knees?
4. Are your heels lower than your toes?
5. Are you close to the saddle at all times?
6. Do you look comfortable and relaxed?

TEST YOUR FORM: ENGLISH

For best results, have a friend snap several pictures of you while you ride. Compare the pictures with the drawing in Figure 6-25 and answer the questions below:

1. Are your hands over, and slightly in front of, your horse's withers?

2. Is your body vertical, except when posting? Is your back straight?

3. Are your heels down at all times? Do your toes turn at a relaxed angle?

4. Is there a straight line from your knee through your toes?

5. Is there a straight line from your elbow to the bit?

6. Are your eyes up and your shoulders back?

7. Do you look comfortable and relaxed?

CHECK YOUR PROGRESS

Skill	Date
Sitting trot without stirrups for three minutes	_____
Posting trot without holding on for three minutes	_____
Quick dismount from the trot	_____
Vault on bareback (optional)	_____
Posting bareback for five minutes	_____
Sitting the trot bareback for five minutes	_____
Rising position bareback for two minutes	_____
Riding on contact at walk, moving hands	_____
Riding on contact at trot with quiet hands	_____

Neck reining with proper leg aids   _____
Riding the diagonal correctly, with change of
    posting diagonal in center at X   _____
Riding a circle   _____

TEST: PART III, CHAPTER 7, LESSONS 5–8

Written Test (*50 points possible; passing grade, 46*)

1. True or false (1 point each):
    a. Sitting the trot without stirrups is excellent for strengthening your seat.
    b. When you sit without stirrups, your heels should be lower than your toes.
    c. To stay with your horse's mouth at the trot, you must hold your hands absolutely still.
    d. Quiet hands are hands which do not pull on the reins and interfere with your horse's mouth.
    e. You should be able to vault onto your horse when riding bareback.
    f. Riding bareback is excellent for developing general riding form.
    g. Staying in the rising position bareback is quite easy.
    h. Sitting the trot bareback is excellent for developing relaxation in your back and legs.
    i. A crop is a short whip. It is used as an aid in controlling the horse.
    j. While you mount, you should hold your crop in your right hand.

k. The crop should be held pointed upwards across the horse's withers.

l. A Western bit is very severe, and a light touch should give you all the control you need.

m. Only Western horses can be trained to neck rein.

n. When you turn the Western horse, you should lean in the saddle.

o. To ride on contact, shorten your reins only until there is a straight line from your horse's mouth to your elbows.

p. To remain on contact at the walk, you must move your hands and arms.

q. The direct rein is usually used alone in turning your horse.

r. In a turn, your hands should direct while your legs drive.

s. A circle is a round figure the width, or diameter, of the ring.

t. You should allow your horse to speed up a little while riding a diagonal.

u. Do not do the bending poles at the posting trot. It's too confusing.

v. If your horse grows excited while bending poles, relax your hands and use your legs more.

w. Unless you can post with both hands on your hips, you should not try to post on contact.

x. If you are using your hands correctly, your horse will be relaxed in the mouth.

y. Always hit your horse hard with the crop before he has a chance to see it in your hand.

2. Define the following terms completely (5 points each):

a. Vault

    b. Neck reining

    c. Riding on contact

    d. The direct rein

    e. The indirect rein

LESSON 9:
DOUBLE REINS; HALTS; HALF-TURN ON FOREHAND

Mount.	
A / Use of double reins. (Optional, English).	
Review of riding on contact (English).	
Practice circles and diagonals.	**10 minutes**
B / The halt.	**15 minutes**
C / Half-turn on forehand.	**10 minutes**
D / Half-halt.	**10 minutes**
Pole-bending.	**15 minutes**
Quick dismount at trot.	

A / Using Double Reins

Double reins are usually associated with bits that give greater control. Pelham and weymouth bridles both have two sets of reins. Many horses are never ridden with double reins: Others may go on a snaffle in the ring, yet require a pelham for control in the open. You should become familiar with the use of double reins; however, it is not necessary or advisable for you to switch your horse permanently to another bridle. You should ride with the bridle which gives you the best, and least severe, control of your mount. You may practice using double reins, or you may merely study the text, and go on to the next subject in this lesson.

Figure 7–33. Double reins should cross before they get to your hands. The snaffle rein should be outside the curb rein and should go in the bottom of your hand. Keep one or two fingers between the reins. Hold both reins together under your thumb when they leave your hand.

Double reins consist of the snaffle (upper) rein, and the curb (lower) rein. The snaffle rein is usually wider than the curb rein. Neither rein should be very wide, or you will find you have too much in your hands. Arrange the reins so that the snaffle rein is outside the curb rein. The snaffle rein should enter your hand either between your little finger and your palm, or between your ring finger and little finger. The curb rein should be separated from the snaffle rein by one or two fingers. Catch both reins under your thumb where they leave your hand. You

Figure 7–34. Anrock is wearing a full hunt bridle. He walks with his head and neck relaxed, as hunters should move. Saddlebred horses will draw their heads up when they are put in a full bridle. The snaffle rein goes in a straight line from Anrock's mouth to the rider's elbows. The curb rein is kept slightly loose and is not used unless Anrock pulls against the snaffle.

should take all four reins up to the same length. Many people suggest that you leave the curb reins slightly loose, as the curbing action of the bit can be severe; they feel you should use the curb only when your mount fails to respond to the snaffle. I think you should experiment a little. Some horses are perfectly relaxed when put on contact with the curb. Others toss their heads, open their mouths, and fight at the slightest touch on the curb rein. Watch your horse's mouth and head, and keep your hands light. You must never be rough when you use a curb; and you *should* never be rough with a snaffle! If your horse seems to fight the bit, refuses to move forward freely, or even tries to rear, take the pelham or curb bit off, and go back to riding with only a snaffle.

B / The Halt

Up to this lesson, English riders have been halting by pulling back slightly on the reins; Western riders have been lifting the reins slightly. A better way for both types of riders to halt is as follows:

1. *English riders:* First increase slightly the action of your legs and squeeze with your thighs and the upper most part of your calves.

Figure 7–35. The rider halts Anrock by bracing her back and fixing her hands. Anrock responds by stopping with his hind legs drawn in under his body. The rider should not pull her calves up when she drops her weight into the saddle. Her reins should be shorter so that she won't need to draw her hands back over the saddle to stop her horse.

In this way you drive your horse's hind legs more under his body, making it easier for him to stop. Then fix your hands: hold them still and no longer follow the action of your horse's head and neck. *Western riders:* Raise your hand slightly to establish contact and then fix your hand.

2. At the same time, drop your weight in the saddle. This term means to brace your thighs and your back. Press only your thighs and knees into the saddle. Do not raise your knees. Don't let your calves draw up. You should stiffen your back so that it no longer follows the movement of your horse. Your sensation should be one of growing much heavier.

3. Hold the above position until your mount stops with all four legs lined up squarely. You should practice feeling the position of his legs under his body. When you think your horse is balanced equally on all four feet, relax your hands and seat. Lean down to check the placement of his legs. This action of looking gives you feedback: You get to check your accuracy. Practicing a skill with feedback is the best way to learn.

4. If the horse fails to stop, increase your contact with his mouth, and try again.

In summary, follow these steps:

1. Tighten your legs slightly.
2. Fix your hands.
3. Drop your weight.
4. Hold your position until the horse stops.
5. Check to see if he stopped with all four legs lined up squarely under his body.

C / Half-turn on the Forehand

The half-turn on the forehand is basically an exercise in coordination for you and your mount. It has little practical value, though you can use it to help in opening gates while mounted. You should never practice the half-turn more than once or twice in each direction, because of the danger of straining your mount's shoulders.

Figure 7–36. The rider is illustrating the aids for the turn on the forehand to the right. Her right hand is lowered, while her left hand is held in its normal position. Her right leg and whip are used behind the girth. The horse is turned from a square halt. A horse cannot do a correct forehand turn if his legs are not lined up under his body.

When he makes a half-turn on the forehand, your horse should hold one forefoot (the pivot foot) immobile. The hind legs and the other foreleg should move around so that the horse turns 180 degrees. He should step neither forward, backward, or to one side. Always turn the haunches away from the rail (for a diagram, see Figure 7-40).

Figure 7–37. Anrock is turning to the right, pivoting around his right fore foot. You can see that his right leg is twisting. His hind legs cross as he steps in a small circle around his right fore leg. The rider can see the ridge above Anrock's right eye. If his head were turned farther to the right, it would be incorrect. The left rein on the neck (left indirect rein) keeps Anrock from pulling his head out of position.

Figure 7–38. Here is another view of the half-turn on the forehand to the right. Anrock has his head bent just the proper amount to the right. His hindquarters are moving to the left.

If you are at a halt at the letter B, and the rail is on your left, you should move your horse's haunches to your right until the rail is on your right, and the horse is standing straight. This is called a half-turn on the forehand to the left. The pivot foot is the horse's left fore.

To make the half-turn, first halt your horse so that his forelegs are lined up as much as possible. Instead of relaxing the reins, keep him on contact! If you make the turn to the left, next lower your left hand. Keep your horse's head straight with your right hand, which should remain in position a few inches above and slightly to the right of the withers. Both reins should touch the horse's neck at its widest point. Western riders should move their rein hand to the left so that the right neck rein is brought into action.

Next, apply your right leg on the girth to keep your horse from stepping backwards. Draw your left leg well behind the girth and tap or kick. If necessary, use the crop on the left side.

Figure 7–39. After the half-turn on the forehand or any difficult exercise, you should let your horse rest on a loose rein. A few pats on the neck relax him and let him know that he has pleased you.

Figure 7–40. Half-turn on the forehand.

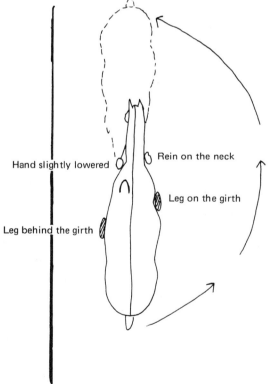

Hand slightly lowered

Rein on the neck

Leg on the girth

Leg behind the girth

Pivot foot

Do not lean in the saddle. Keep your weight balanced in the saddle and use your reins and legs to cause the horse to move his hindquarters to the right. This exercise will be difficult for you at first. You should practice a little each lesson until you can do it perfectly in both directions.

In summary, follow these directions:

1. Halt.
2. Lower your left hand.
3. Hold the right rein steady.
4. Apply your right leg on the girth, your left leg behind the girth.
5. Reverse the aids for a half-turn to the right.

D / The Half-Halt

The half-halt is used to raise the horse's head, and to cause him to carry more of his weight on his hind-quarters. We will use it to obtain a smooth canter depart in later lessons. You may consider a half-halt to be half of a halt.

To half-halt, follow these steps:

1. Practice from a walk.

Figure 7–41. This picture was taken at the moment of the half-halt. The rider has dropped her weight and fixed her hands. Anrock is responding by bringing his head back and rounding his hind legs under his body. The rider should not have her heels up in this exercise.

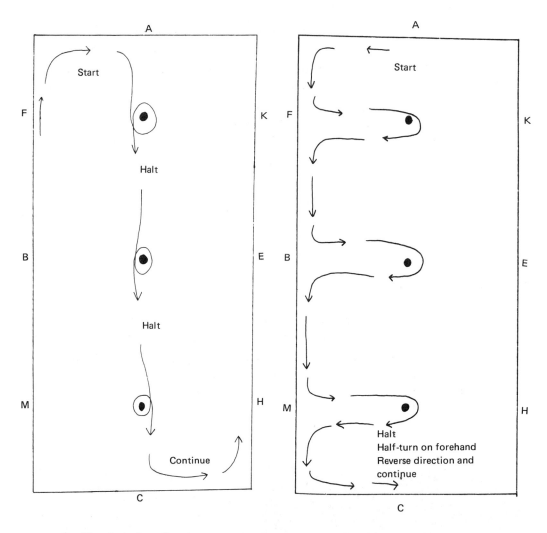

Figure 7–42. Pole bending III.   **Figure 7–43.** Pole bending IV.

2. Prepare to halt.

3. Fix your hands and drop your weight into the saddle.

4. An instant before your horse comes to a full halt, drive him forward with your legs.

Your sensation should be one of a slight, but definite, hesitation in stride.

PRACTICE RIDE 3

Letter	Movement
A	Begin at walk. English riders should be on contact. Go to the left on the track.
E	Begin the sitting trot.
C	Circle the width of the ring.
C	Sit the trot on the track to K.
K–X–M	Ride the diagonal.
C	English riders begin posting.
H–X–F	Ride the diagonal. English riders change posting diagonals at X.
E	Trot posting to E. Walk at E.
C	Halt. Half-turn on forehand.
C	Walk.
H	Half-halt.
E	Half-halt.
K	Halt. Half-turn on forehand.
K	Walk.
E	Trot, sitting.
C	Circle width of ring.
C	Trot posting.
A	Walk.
E	Halt.

LESSON 10:
SCHOOL FIGURES II

Mount.

Practice circles and diagonals.   **10 minutes**

Practice riding on contact.		
Review half-turn on forehand.	**10 minutes**	
Review halt and half-halt.	**5 minutes**	
A / **Half-circle and half-circle in reverse.**	**15 minutes**	
B / **Turn through the ring.**	**5 minutes**	
C / **Serpentine.**	**5 minutes**	
D / **Cavaletti.**	**10 minutes**	
Dismount.		

A / Half-Circle and Half-Circle in Reverse

HALF-CIRCLE

You may think of the half-circle as half a circle. The circle, in this case, is the small circle with a diameter half the width of the ring. The half-circle is used to reverse direction, and to improve the responsiveness of the horse. It is also an excellent exercise to improve the coordination of the rider.

Half-circles are performed at letters F,B,M,K,E and H. You cannot do a half-circle at A or C. The most instructive gait for this exercise is the sitting trot. You may ride half-circles at the walk. Later, you will learn to ride them at the canter.

To make a half-circle (for example, at H) follow these steps (see Figures 7-44—46).

1. Approach H from E along the track.

2. When your shoulder is even with H, begin a small circle. Your circle should touch the center line at 180 degrees to H. You should ride a perfect semi-circle. Mark the point on the center line with a marker, if necessary.

3. Straighten your horse, and ride to E at a 45 degree angle. You should ride a straight line to E with no wavering. Enter the track so that the horse's shoulder is by E when he steps onto the track.

Use the following aids for steps 1, 2, and 3:

1. Prepare your horse for the turn by pressing the points of your buttocks into the saddle and increasing your pressure on the reins slightly.

2. Turn, using either the direct and indirect reins or the neck rein. Use your inside leg on the girth and your outside leg behind the girth. Push with your seat (press with the points of your buttocks). Do not lean backwards, forwards, or in any other direction. Do not raise either hand above its normal position.

3. To straighten your horse, switch your legs so that the outside leg is on the girth and the inside leg is behind the girth. Hold your hands steady so that the horse feels equal pressure from both reins. Thus, you reverse direction, or "change hands."

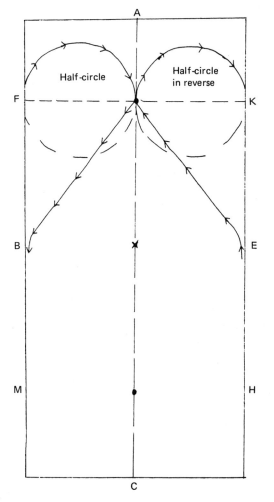

Figure 7–44. Half-circle and half-circle in reverse.

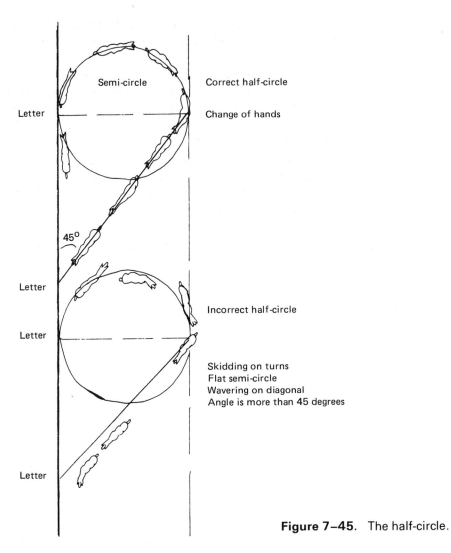

Figure 7–45. The half-circle.

HALF-CIRCLE IN REVERSE

The half-circle in reverse is the half-circle ridden from the diagonal into the circle rather than from the circle into the diagonal to the track. It is slightly more difficult than a half-circle. Again, you might mark a point on the center line 180 degrees from H to help you in judging your distances.

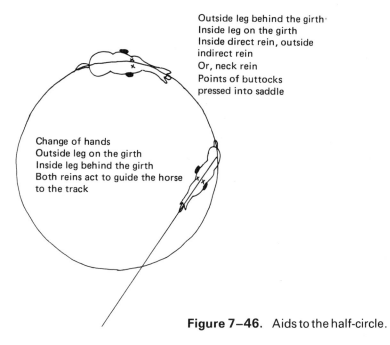

Outside leg behind the girth·
Inside leg on the girth
Inside direct rein, outside
indirect rein
Or, neck rein
Points of buttocks
pressed into saddle

Change of hands
Outside leg on the girth
Inside leg behind the girth
Both reins act to guide the horse
to the track

Figure 7–46. Aids to the half-circle.

To make a half-circle in reverse (for example, from E to H) follow these steps (see Figures 7–47 and 7–48):

1. Approach E from K along the track.

2. When your shoulder is even with E, leave the track at a 45 degree angle.

3. When you reach the center line (180 degrees from H), ride a semi-circle to H. You will re-enter the track at H, moving towards E.

Use the following aids for steps 1, 2, and 3:

1. Prepare your horse for the turn by pressing the points of your buttocks into the saddle and increasing your pressure on the reins slightly.

2. Use either the neck rein or the direct and indirect reins to guide your horse off the track.

3. Put your horse into the turn by using the neck rein or the direct and indirect reins. Push with your seat, and use your inside leg on the girth, your outside leg behind the girth. At H, again straighten your horse.

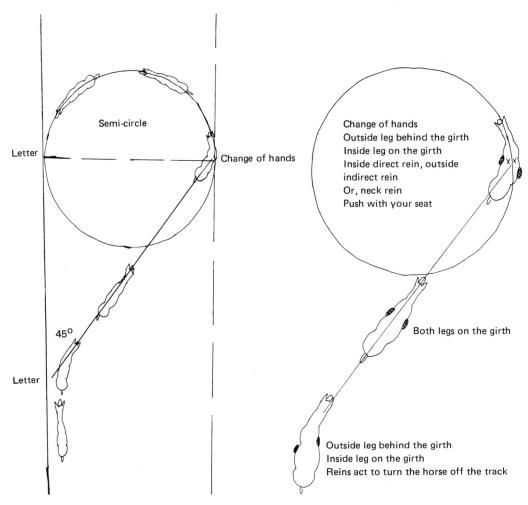

Figure 7–47. The half-circle in reverse.

Figure 7–48. Aids to the half-circle in re-verse.

B / Turn Through the Ring

Until this lesson, you have turned through the ring at random. If you wanted to cut across the ring, you did so. Sometimes you changed direction on the turn; sometimes you did not. From this lesson on, however, a "turn through the ring" will usually refer to either the turn across the mid-line, or the turn down the center line. Either turn may call for a change in direction of movement on the track. In this case, the turns will be called the reverse across the mid-line, or the reverse down the center line.

The mid-line is a straight line drawn from B to E. The center line is a straight line drawn from C to A. If it helps you, you may mark these lines with agricultural lime.

To make either turn, follow this procedure (see Figures 7–49 and 7–50):

1. Prepare to turn as you approach the letter.
2. Before you reach the letter, start your turn. Your horse should

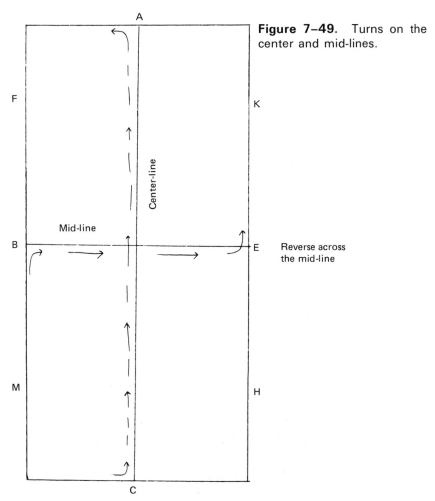

Figure 7–49. Turns on the center and mid-lines.

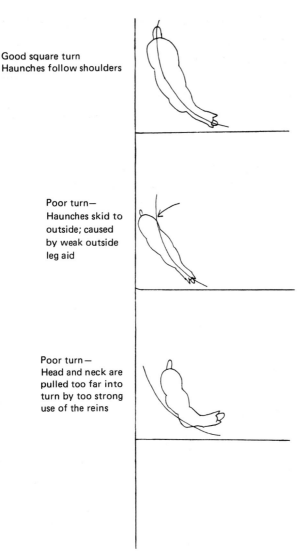

Good square turn
Haunches follow shoulders

Poor turn—
Haunches skid to
outside; caused
by weak outside
leg aid

Poor turn—
Head and neck are
pulled too far into
turn by too strong
use of the reins

Figure 7–50.   Square turns.

leave the track on the line! It is not correct to overshoot or under-shoot, and then swerve onto the line.

3. While riding on the mid-line or the center line, keep your eyes trained on the letter at the other side or end of the ring. You must ride an absolutely straight line with no wavering.

4. Start turning as you approach the track so that you have room for a smooth turn. You should not slow down or allow your horse to skid with his hindquarters on these turns.

5. Do not post in this exercise. Stay down in the saddle. Use your legs and drop your weight down in the saddle on the turns. Don't haul your mount around with your hands.

C / Serpentine

The serpentine is a series of loops down the ring. The number of loops in a serpentine will vary with the abilities of the horse and rider. You may make one, three, or five loops; however, all loops should be equal in size in any one serpentine. This exercise is used to increase your riding skills and to improve the responsiveness of your horse.

You may start a serpentine at letters F,M,K or H. In this example, we will start at K. Follow these steps (see Figures 7-51 and 7-52):

1. Approach K through the turn.

2. At K, turn and ride a straight line to a point on the track mid-way between F and B.

3. At the track, turn and ride a straight line to E.

4. At E, turn and ride a straight line to a point on the track midway between B and M.

5. At the track, turn and ride a straight line to H.

6. At H, stay on the track and ride through the corner.

You should take care not to skid your horse on the turns, and not to allow your mount to waver on the straight lines. Ride at the walk or the sitting trot. In case you do not understand what I mean by "skidding" or "wavering" let me take a moment to explain. Your horse skids when he swings his hind end out. For example, you are riding a circle. Your horse should have his back bent so his body is round like the circle. If he throws his hind legs out and tries to circle without bending his back, he is said to "skid" (another term sometimes used is to "range the haunches").

To keep your horse from skidding, you must use your legs. Both legs are important, but your outside leg behind the girth is most important. This leg makes your horse bend his back and keeps him from skidding his hind legs out of the circle.

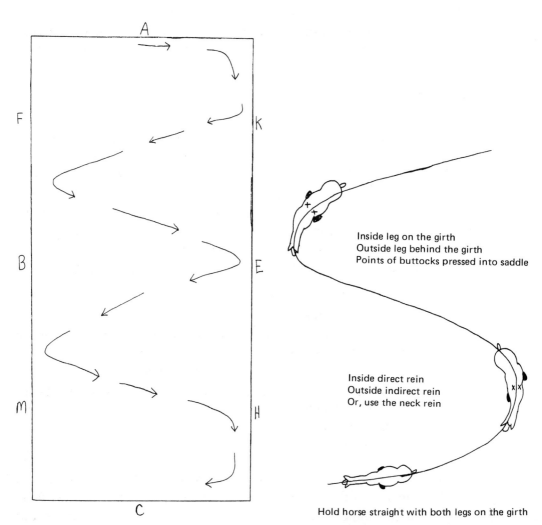

Inside leg on the girth
Outside leg behind the girth
Points of buttocks pressed into saddle

Inside direct rein
Outside indirect rein
Or, use the neck rein

Hold horse straight with both legs on the girth

Figure 7-51. The serpentine.   **Figure 7-52.** Aids for the serpentine.

Your horse wavers not on circles but on straight lines. For example, if you are riding up the center line in the ring, you should be riding a straight line. Your horse is wavering if he weaves from one side to the other.

To keep your horse from wavering, use both your legs on the girth. Push both your legs into your horse's sides to drive him forward. He cannot move from side to side and strongly forward at the same time. By driving him forward, you help keep him moving on a straight line.

D / Cavaletti

PURPOSE OF THE CAVALETTI

The cavaletti are a series of low obstacles used to teach a horse to space his strides evenly, and to introduce him to jumping. They are also useful in teaching guidance and control to the rider. All students should practice the cavaletti.

INTRODUCTION TO THE CAVALETTI

If your horse is not familiar with the cavaletti, you should give him an introductory lesson. Set the cavaletti in place, and lead him to them. Let him sniff the rails, then lead him across. Most horses will respond without fear after a few minutes of careful, patient introduction. If your horse acts terrified or panicked, skip both the cavaletti and the jumping sections of these lessons.

Some horses bruise badly when they rap their legs on cavaletti rails. You may protect your mount with polo boots and bell boots, or you may wrap his legs in stable bandages. Usually, wraps on the front legs provide enough protection.

Figure 7-53. Chocolate is walking through a cavaletti made of jump rails placed in concrete blocks. The blocks keep the rails from rolling. She is correctly walking through the middle of the cavaletti on firm contact. Even Western riders should have their reins fairly short when they introduce cavaletti work. Keep your horse under control but do not pull on his mouth. Keep your legs tight so that he will move forward in a straight line.

SAFETY PRECAUTIONS

Use only cavaletti constructed as those shown in the first section of this book. Logs or rails laid upon the ground are dangerous as they roll when they are touched. Wear a hard hat if you ride in an English saddle. Don't practice unless someone is around who can if necessary help you.

If you can persuade him, a friend can serve as your helper and save you much time. Have him stand by to move the cavaletti as you adjust the spacing.

SPACING AND HEIGHT

For practice at the walk and trot, set seven cavaletti in a row. The rails should be six to ten inches off the ground. Set them about four to five feet apart to start, then adjust them to fit the stride of your mount.

Your horse should step over one cavaletti rail in each stride. If he clears more than one, move the rails farther apart. If he knocks the rails and stumbles, you may need to move the rails closer together. Your friend can watch and set the rails as necessary. If you have no assistant, you must continue to dismount and move the rails until the horse goes through the cavaletti smoothly without knocking the wood.

HOW TO RIDE THROUGH CAVALETTI

Follow these steps (see Figure 7-54):

1. Begin at the walk. Your horse should be on contact (English) or on fairly short, but not tight, reins (Western).

2. Approach at a 90 degree angle to the middle of the cavaletti. Aim for the exact center of the rails.

3. Maintain an even pace. Do not allow your horse to hesitate or rush as he enters the cavaletti.

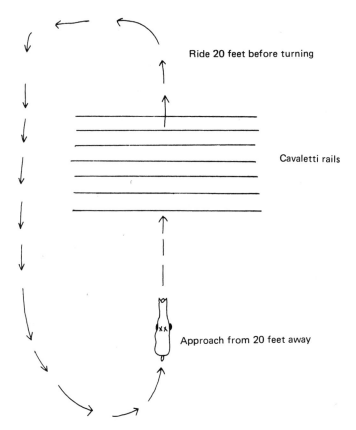

Ride 20 feet before turning

Cavaletti rails

Approach from 20 feet away

Use both legs on the girth and your seat to maintain a straight,
even approach

Figure 7-54. Cavaletti I.

4. Ride a straight line through the cavaletti. Maintain an even pace. Remain in the saddle. Do not lean forward, but use your seat to push your horse at an even rate of speed.

5. Ride straight after leaving the cavaletti for 20 feet.

6. Circle back to 20 feet in front of the cavaletti, and approach again.

7. Walk through five to ten times. Then trot the cavaletti five to ten times. Approach at, and maintain, a slow, even trot.

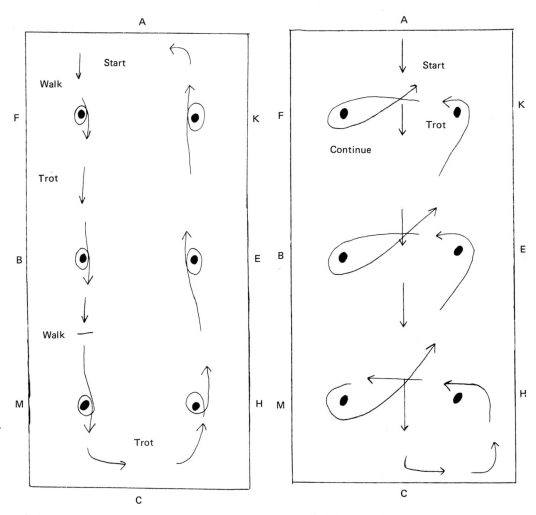

Figure 7–55. Pole bending V.   **Figure 7–56.** Pole bending VI.

PRACTICE RIDE 4

Letter	*Movement*
A	Begin at walk. English, on contact. Track left.
E	Halt, half-turn on forehand to right.
E	Walk.
B	Halt. Half-turn on forehand to left.
B	Walk.
F	Half-halt.
A	Trot, sitting.
H	Half-circle.
E	Trot sitting to M. Half-circle at M.
A	Post.
K–X–M	Trot the diagonal. English riders change posting diagonals at X.
C	Sit the trot.
E	Reverse across the ring to B.
B	Track right.
F	Half-circle to B.
B	Trot sitting to H.
H	Half-circle in reverse to E.
C	Walk.
B	Halt.

LESSON 11:
REIN-BACK AND CANTER

Mount.

Review of school figures.   **25 minutes**

A / Rein-back.   **10 minutes**

B / Canter.   **25 minutes**

    Dismount.

A / Rein-back

The rein-back, also called "to back the horse," is not difficult if done correctly on a trained horse. Even untrained horses can usually be caused to rein-back by skilled application of the aids. As you remember, your aids for controlling your horse are your hands, your legs, and your seat.

In the rein-back, the horse walks backwards. His legs move in diagonal pairs, as in a trot, but with no period of suspension (see Figure 7-59). The horse should move in regularly spaced steps, without hesitation or rushing. The hindlegs should remain in line with the forelegs: the horse should not spread his hindlegs apart, or move them to one side. In a good rein-back,

Figure 7–57. Anrock is reining-back correctly. He is moving his legs as diagonal pairs and going backward calmly and straight. His head is in the correct position, neither above nor behind the bit.

Figure 7–58. Chocolate decided to illustrate an improper rein-back. She has her nose in the air and is fighting every step of the way. She is stepping back one foot at a time, rather than by diagonal pairs.

the horse will not raise his head or open his mouth. You should be able to rein-back for three smooth strides without stopping.

To rein-back, follow these steps:

1. First, halt so that your mount is balanced over all four legs. Keep your horse on contact (English).

2. Drop your weight in the saddle. Do not lean backwards, but press the points of your buttocks into the saddle. Tighten your thighs without pulling up your calves.

3. Apply a fixed pressure on the reins. Do not jerk backwards! Jerking may cause your horse to step back, but he will raise his head and back incorrectly.

4. Your horse should yield to the bit and to your legs. He should relax his jaw and step backwards calmly without resistance. If he does not back, increase your pressure on the reins, and try again. Press with your calves to urge him to move backward. It may be necessary for you to vibrate the reins a little with your fingers. Vibrating the reins will encourage your horse to relax his jaw and yield to your demands. Do not jerk or pull. Western riders should lift their hand gently once or twice. English riders should open and close their fingers a few times.

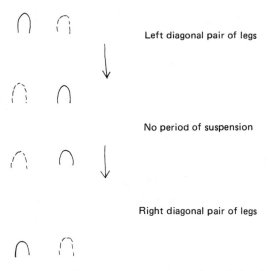

Left diagonal pair of legs

No period of suspension

Right diagonal pair of legs

Figure 7–59. Leg movement in the rein-back.

5. Do not lean backwards or forwards at any time. Do not jerk or saw with the reins. Keep your weight pushed into the saddle, and keep your back straight. The only movement you should do is to vibrate the reins gently, if necessary.

B / Canter

DEFINITION OF THE CANTER

A canter is a slow, controlled gallop. As such, it is a three-beat gait. The sequence of leg movement can be either left hind-leg, left diagonal (right hind and left foreleg), right foreleg, suspension; or right hindleg, right diagonal, left foreleg, suspension (see Figure 7-60). Note that a canter stride begins with one hindleg, and ends with a point of suspension during which no legs are on the ground.

A horse may canter on either the right or the left lead. The first sequence described above is the canter on the right lead; the second sequence is the canter on the left lead. The word "lead" refers to the action of the forelegs. On the right lead, the right foreleg actually moves farther to the front than the left foreleg. It seems to lead the horse.

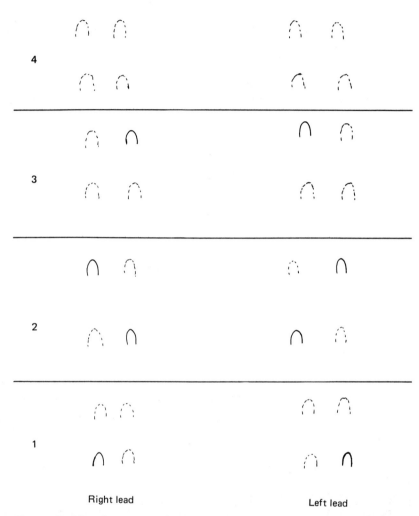

Right lead   Left lead

Figure 7–60. Sequence of legs at the canter.

At first you will have trouble telling the leads apart. You should learn to tell by the feel of the strides: The right lead will toss you slightly to the right, and the left lead will make you move to the left. However, you will need to watch your mount's shoulders at first, or have a friend tell you which lead you are riding. To tell from watching the shoulders, you must know that the leading shoulder always moves farther to the front than the shoulder of the non-leading leg. Also, if you lean forward slightly, you will be able to see the leading leg extending beyond the non-leading leg as they stretch in front of your mount. Always guess before you look. Guessing, with the feedback of looking, will help you develop feel.

Sometimes horses scramble their strides, leading on, for example, the right on the front, while cross-cantering on the back. The sequence of steps in this example will be right hind, left hind; left fore, and right fore. It is a rough, four-beat gait. If you feel your horse suddenly become extremely rough, he has probably switched to this gait. You should return to the trot and start over.

RIDER'S SENSATIONS

The canter will move you in ways different from the movements of the walk or the trot. You will be tossed backwards and forwards, and up and down. Your only defense is to relax! If you stiffen your back, you will bounce.

FORM AT THE CANTER

You should sit as you did for the walk and the sitting trot. Your back should be straight, your shoulders square, your head up, and your knees pushed well downwards. You must absorb

Figure 7-61. The rider is showing fair form at the canter on loose reins. The reins are loose, even though they are not hanging. The rider's legs are out of position, as her toes are too far forward.

Figure 7–62. Many beginners sit at the canter like the rider in the picture. They lean forward, hang off the reins, and bounce. You should hang onto the saddle or the mane and force your seat down until you learn to sit the canter. Chocolate is moving on the left lead.

the movements of the canter in the small of your back. Do not lean backwards, but do try to keep your seat pressed well down into the saddle. Your knees and thighs should be against the saddle, while your calves should be relaxed, and your heels lower than your toes.

The horse moves his head a lot when he canters. You must be very relaxed and supple to follow correctly with your hands. Therefore, I suggest that you put your horse on a loose rein at first, until you develop your balance. Don't be ashamed to grab hold of the mane or the saddle.

CANTER DEPART WITHOUT REGARD TO THE LEAD

I am going to outline two ways to put your horse into a canter (For aids to the canter, see Figure 7-63). The first is more correct; the second may be easier. Try the first. If it doesn't work, use the second.

Method 1:

1. Put your horse into a slow trot. English horses should be on contact.

2. As you approach the turn in the corner of the ring, prepare to canter.

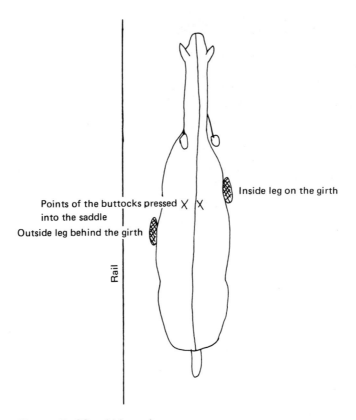

Figure 7-63. Aids to the canter.

3. As you come out of the turn, straighten your horse, do a half-halt to gather your mount slightly.

4. Immediately release the pressure on the reins. At the same time, press your legs into your horse. The leg by the rail should kick behind the girth; the leg away from the rail should tighten on the girth.

5. If you kick and release properly, your horse will canter. If you release the reins too soon, he will speed his trot. If you release too late, he will try to canter but be frustrated by your hands. You will feel him come up a little on the front end, and then continue at the trot. Slow the trot and try again.

6. Once he is cantering, hang on and concentrate on your seat. Try to keep him on the track. Otherwise, he will run into the center of the ring and stop. If he tries to drop from the canter, tap or kick with

your outside heel (the one closest to the rail). If he tries to run into the ring, use your inside heel to keep him on the track.

Method 2:

1. Put your horse into a slow trot on a loose rein.
2. Grab the mane or the saddle.
3. Say "Canter!" and kick with both heels. Use only your heels. Do not draw your knees from the saddle. Some horses will canter better if you use only your outside heel. Use the heels behind the girth.
4. Your horse will probably begin to trot very fast. Keep after him with your heels until he canters. If necessary, use the crop on the outside, behind the girth.
5. Do not, at any time, lean forward. Once your horse begins to canter, follow Number 6 in Method 1 above.
6. Now try the first method of aids to the canter. The first method takes more coordination on your part; however, if you can perform it, you will get a much smoother transition from a trot to a canter, and be much more comfortable.

Once you begin to develop your seat at the canter, you should try some in-saddle exercises to help develop your relaxation. Try circling your feet, or riding without stirrups. Don't forget to practice developing your feel for the leads. Guess which lead your horse is cantering before you look at his shoulders.

You can canter large circles in the ring. Your horse might try to throw his haunches out on the turns. Keep him straight by pressing with your outside leg behind the girth. If he slows his gait on the circle, kick with your inside leg behind the girth, and press with your seat. Check your hands to make sure you are not pulling him out of the canter by too much pressure on the reins.

Do not attempt to ride the canter on contact until your seat is secure. It is difficult to canter on contact without jerking the horse's mouth because horses move their heads quite a bit at this gait.

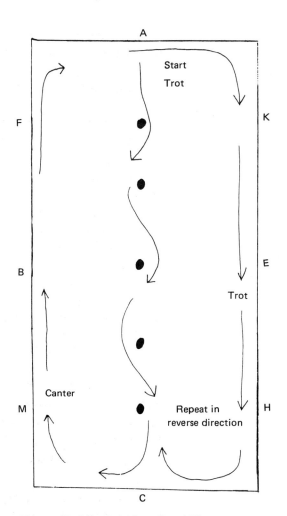

Figure 7–65 Pole bending VII.

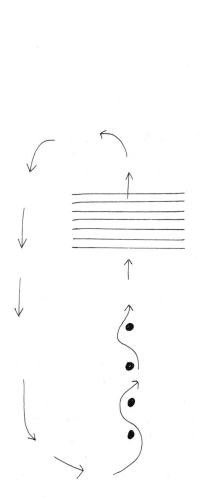

Figure 7–64. Cavaletti II: Set the poles at least 20 feet from the cavaletti and about 20 feet apart. Ride at the walk or the trot. The poles should be set in a straight line at a 90-degree angle from the center of the first cavaletti rail.

PRACTICE RIDE 5

Letter	Movement
A	Enter, walk. English riders on contact. Track left.
E	Trot, sitting.
M	Serpentine to F.
K–X–M	Ride the diagonal.
H	Serpentine to K.
A	Post the trot.
B	Ride circle, width of the ring.
B	Sit the trot.
A	Turn up the center line.
X	Halt.

PRACTICE RIDE 6

Letter	Movement
A	Enter, walk. English riders on contact. Track up the center line.
X	Halt. Count to five. Continue at walk.
C	Track right.
M	Trot. English riders post.
B	Circle, width of ring.
B	Continue trotting on track.
K–X–M	Ride diagonal. English riders change posting diagonals at X.
H–X–F	Ride diagonal. English riders change posting diagonals at X.
E	Walk.
C	Halt. Rein-back three steps. Walk.

M	Trot, sitting. Ride on the track to C.
C–M	Pick up the canter on the turn between C and M.
B	Circle width of the ring.
B	Continue at canter on the track.
E	Trot. English riders post.
B	Reverse across the mid-line.
E	Track left. Sit the trot.
C–H	Pick up the canter on the turn between C and H.
B	Circle, width of the ring.
B	Continue at the canter on the track.
E	Trot. English riders post.
A	Walk on a loose rein.

PRACTICE RIDE 7

Letter	Movement
A	Enter at walk. English riders on contact. Walk up center line.
X	Halt. Count to five. Continue at walk.
C	Track right.
B	Halt. Rein-back three steps. Continue at walk.
A	Trot. English riders post.
B	Sit the trot.
K	Serpentine to H. Continue on the track to the right.
A–K	Pick up the canter between A and K. Canter once around the ring.
E	Trot. English riders post.
M–X–K	Trot the diagonal. English riders change posting diagonals at X.
B	Sit the trot.
C–H	Pick up the canter between C and H. Canter once around the ring.
E	Trot. English riders post.
A	Walk, loose rein.

LESSON 12: TRAIL RIDE

Go on a ride along the trails.   **60–180 minutes**

Riding the trails is fun. It's an interesting way to break up your practice sessions, so that you don't spend all your riding hours in a dusty ring. If you have friends who ride, you may go on the trails in company long before this lesson. The friends will watch out for you, and help you if you get into trouble. However, if you are riding alone, you should wait to go out until you can sit the canter to some degree. For your own safety, you should not canter your horse on the trail until you have finished all the lessons in this book. Then you will be able to stay on and control your horse well enough at this gait to avoid accidents. I suggest that you learn to ride the canter a little before you go on the trail alone because your horse might surprise you when you get him on the trail. Some horses that are very calm in the ring grow very eager when they see wide-open spaces. Your horse might boldly go into a canter when you aren't expecting it. If you have ridden the canter, you will not be upset. You will know how to easily bring your mount back to the trot or the walk. However, if you have never experienced the canter, you might rightfully feel afraid. This is a particular danger if you are by yourself. More experienced rider companions can help you control your horse by giving you advice, and by keeping their own mounts moving at slow paces.

Following are several rules for trail riding. If you abide by these rules, you will be less likely to be hurt or frightened on the trails (also see Chapter 8 on potential problems).

1. Use a saddle and bridle. Don't ride with a halter. Don't go on the trail bareback yet.

2. Wear proper riding clothing. English riders should wear hard hats. You are more, not less, likely to be hurt out of the ring.

3. Choose quiet trails. Don't ride along busy highways or motor-

bike paths. If you have no horse trails or back country roads, stay home and ride in the ring.

4. Ride at a walk. Trot only on soft ground away from distractions. Don't trot towards the barn.

5. If a car approaches, get as far from the road as possible. If your horse acts at all alarmed, or if some strange noisy vehicle approaches, stop and turn your mount to face it. If necessary, get off.

6. If your horse refuses to pass an obstacle or cross a bridge or puddle, drive him with your legs and the crop. If it seems a fight will develop, get off and lead him past. Don't turn back: He will probably be worse the next time. Do not fight with him. You are not yet an experienced enough rider to weather a fight.

7. If your mount should start or shy, do not punish him. Punishment will make him more upset. Calm him by patting him on the neck.

8. If you are with other riders, follow these guidelines:

   a. Never ride directly in front of or behind another horse. Your horse might kick, or be kicked.

   b. Never change gait without warning the other riders. Tell them your plans and give them time to get their mounts under control before you change gait.

   c. Never trot up behind another group of horses. Your horse might get kicked, or he might frighten the other horses.

   d. Always warn other riders before you pass them on the trail. Let them know you are coming up behind them. Then pass at a sane gait. Never gallop past other horses. The horses will become very upset if you do and might cause injury to someone.

TEST YOUR FORM: WESTERN

For best results, have a friend snap several pictures of you while you ride. Then compare the pictures to the drawing in Figure 6-26. Answer the questions below.

1. Are your arms in a straight line with your body?
2. Are you sitting straight in the saddle?
3. Are your toes even with, or just slightly to the front of, your knees?
4. Are your heels lower than your toes?
5. Are you close to the saddle at all times?
6. Do you look comfortable and relaxed?

TEST YOUR FORM: ENGLISH

For best results, have a friend snap several pictures of you while you ride. Compare the pictures to the drawing in Figure 6-25. Then answer the questions below.

1. Are your hands over, and slightly in front of, your horse's withers?
2. Is your body vertical, except when posting? Is your back straight?
3. Are your heels down at all times? Do your toes turn at a relaxed angle?
4. Is there a straight line from your knee through your toes?
5. Is there a straight line from your elbow to the bit?
6. Are your eyes up and your shoulders back?
7. Do you look comfortable and relaxed?

CHECK YOUR PROGRESS

Skill	Date
Half-turn on forehand to the right	————
Half-turn on forehand to the left	————
The halt, using your weight	————
The half-halt at the walk	————
Half-circle, without skidding	————
Half-circle in reverse, without skidding or ranging haunches	————
Turn across the mid-line, without skidding	————
Serpentine	————
Cavaletti at walk	————
Cavaletti at trot	————
Rein-back three steps	————
Canter depart using half-halt	————
Able to tell right and left leads by looking at shoulder	————
Able to tell right and left leads without looking	————
Trail ride	————

TEST: PART III, CHAPTER 7, LESSONS 9–12

Written Test (50 points possible; passing grade, 46)

1. True or false (1 point each)
    a. Double reins are usually associated with bits that give greater control.
    b. To halt, first tighten your legs a little to bring your horse's hind legs more under his body.

    c. "Drop your weight" means to lean backwards.

    d. When he makes a half-turn on the forehand, your horse pivots about one hind foot.

    e. The half-halt is used to raise the horse's head, and to cause him to carry more of his weight on his hindquarters.

    f. A half-circle is half a circle.

    g. Half-circles can be performed at letters A and C.

    h. The mid-line is a straight line drawn from B to E.

    i. The serpentine is a series of loops down the ring.

    j. You may start a serpentine at any letter.

    k. Cavaletti is a series of low obstacles used to teach a horse to space his strides evenly.

    l. Logs laid on the ground make a good cavaletti.

    m. Set up five cavaletti seven feet apart.

    n. The rein-back is also called "to back the horse."

    o. In the rein-back, the horse trots backwards.

    p. To rein-back you should jerk and saw with the reins.

    q. A canter is a slow, controlled gallop.

    r. The sequence of beats in the right lead is left hindleg, left diagonal, right foreleg.

    s. To ride the canter, you should lean forward into the rising position.

    t. Cantering on contact is very difficult.

    u. You may dress as you please while you trail ride.

    v. Always trot towards the barn on the trail.

    w. Never dismount while on the trail.

    x. If your horse should jump or shy, beat him with your crop.

2. Define these terms (5 points each):

    a. Half-circle in reverse

b. Reverse down the center line

c. Skid on the turn

d. Leads at the canter

e. Aids to a canter depart

LESSON 13:
STARTS AND STOPS;
SCHOOL FIGURES III

Mount.	
Review (Practice Ride).	15 minutes
Review the canter.	15 minutes
A / **Starts and stops to the trot from the halt.**	5 minutes
B / **Small circles and figure eights.**	10 minutes
C / **Broken lines.**	5 minutes
D / **Broken lines with quarter-turn on the haunches.**	10 minutes
Dismount.	

A / Starts and Stops to the Trot from the Halt

Until now, you should have always halted from the walk, and trotted from the walk. Now I am going to discuss halting from the trot, and trotting from the halt. Both these exercises call for more control of your mount, and greater coordination of your aids—the hands, the legs, the seat.

To halt from the trot, first prepare to halt. Choose a spot in the ring (for example, letter C) and plan to halt so that your shoulder is beside the letter. A few strides before the letter, increase the tension in your seat and thighs slightly. This action will get your mount's attention. Then, allowing yourself a few strides to halt, fix your hands and drop your weight into the saddle. The number of strides you will need for a complete halt depends upon the responsiveness of your mount, and the skill you possess. Do not make a fast stop at the expense of form. Your horse should stop smoothly, without tossing his head or skidding with his hind legs. He should stop so that he is balanced over all four of his legs. Ideally, he should take no strides of the walk between the trot and the halt; however, don't become angry or frustrated if he does walk a step or two. You might need several hours of practice before you are able to get a good halt.

To trot from the halt, again you must first get your mount's attention. English horses should be on contact; all horses should be alerted by a tightening of the muscles in your seat and thighs, and by slight vibrations of the reins. When your horse is alert, tap sharply with both heels to send him into the trot. The strength of the tap will depend upon the responsiveness of your mount. Some horses will trot out if you increase the tension in your calves; others will require a rap with the crop. It is important that your horse be standing balanced over all four legs before you ask for the trot. Otherwise, he will not be able to begin the trot smoothly, without jerking, or walking. Faults you may encounter include taking strides of the walk, dragging his hind legs at the start, rushing forward, and coming up on the front as if to canter. You should practice until you can get a smooth transition from the halt to the walk. The first three faults can be corrected by balancing your horse before you ask, and by driving him forward with light tension on the reins. The last fault is usually caused by too powerful an application of the aids. Relax your horse. Even if he walks a stride or two before he trots, he will eventually learn to trot smoothly from a halt.

B / Small Circles and Figure Eights

A small circle is a circle with a diameter half the width of the ring (see Figure 7-66). You may make small circles at any letter; however, you will find them easier to make on the letters

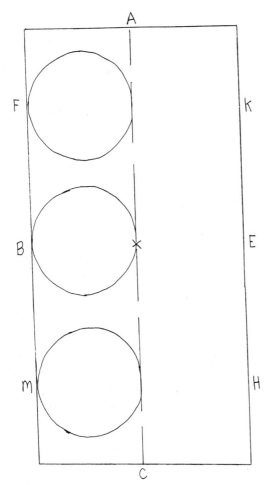

Figure 7–66. Small circles.

other than A and C. Along the sides of the ring you will be able to measure the circumference of the circle by riding to the center line.

To ride a small circle, begin a half-circle. At the center line, ride another semi-circle back to the track. Your small circle should be absolutely round. Your mount should neither slow nor speed his pace. It is a bad fault if he throws his haunches in or out of the circle, or skids with his hind legs. You must use strong leg and seat aids to get a good circle.

A figure eight is merely two small circles strung together (see Figures 7–67 and 7–68). Begin a half-circle at any letter along the side of the ring. When you come to the center line, straighten your mount for three strides. He should be trotting absolutely straight down the center line. Then, make a small circle: from the center line to the track on the other side of the ring, and back to the center line. Again, straighten your horse for three strides. Finally, make a semi-circle back to the track. Done correctly, both small circles in the figure eight will be the same size, and will be perfectly round. This figure will take a lot of practice to do correctly. If necessary, you may draw it into the ring with agricultural lime, or mark the center line and the diameters of the circles with wooden markers.

Figure 7–67. Figure eights.   **Figure 7–68.** Figure eight along the rail.

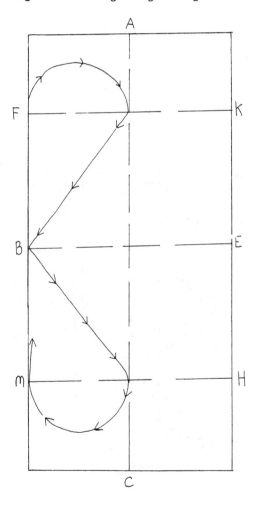

C / Broken Lines

Broken lines are similar to serpentines except for these two differences: Broken lines extend no farther into the ring than the center line; and, the turns in broken lines are much sharper—usually a full 90 degrees. For an example, let's say you are trotting on the track to the right. You are moving from the letter B towards the letter A. You trot past A to K. At K, you turn sharply into the ring at an angle of 90 degrees. Trot to the center line, then turn back towards the track at an angle of 90 degrees. You make first a right turn, then a left turn. When you reach the track, you make another right turn of 90 degrees.

Figure 7–69. In a square turn to the right, the rider uses her right leg on the girth, her left leg behind the girth, and her weight down in the saddle. The left rein is against Anrock's neck, while the right is pulled back and out to move Anrock sharply to the right. Notice that the rider's hands are no farther apart than they are normally. They are simply shifted to the right. Anrock is turning as a unit. His hind legs are following in the track of his forelegs, and his head is bent only slightly in the direction of his motion.
Figure 7–70. Aids for a square turn.

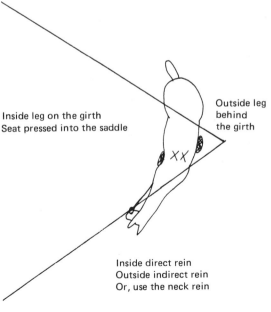

Inside leg on the girth
Seat pressed into the saddle

Outside leg
behind
the girth

Inside direct rein
Outside indirect rein
Or, use the neck rein

Continue making right and left turns until you reach H. At H, you go back to trotting on the track. The sharp turns in broken lines can be done either of two ways: You may move on square turns; or, you may perform quarter-turns on the haunches. To perform square turns, keep your horse moving forward at a trot. Do not slow your pace. A square turn is achieved with the aids you use on any other turn (direct and indirect rein or neck rein, inside leg on the girth, outside leg behind the girth). You must use your legs and seat very strongly and drive your mount into the turn. Use as much rein as necessary to make the turn, but do not haul your horse around with your hands. Rather, drive him around with your legs (see Figure 7-70 for aids). Ideally, he should flow around the turns smoothly without resistance (tossing his head, opening his mouth, pulling to one side) or hesitation. Practice broken lines equally in each direction. You will probably find that your horse moves more easily in one direction than in the other. This difference is to be expected; it will disappear with practice.

D / Broken Lines with Quarter-turn on the Haunches

The other way to work on broken lines is to turn with quarter-turns on the haunches (see Figure 7-71).

To do a quarter-turn on the haunches, first prepare your mount a stride or two before you ask for the exercise. Get his attention by tightening your seat and thighs, and by increasing the tension on the reins slightly. You want him to begin shifting his weight to his hind legs. You may do a half-halt. Next, begin the turn by shifting your own weight backwards sharply. Do not lean backwards, but drop your weight into the saddle by resisting with your back, tightening your thighs, and pressing the points of your buttocks into the saddle. Press both your calves into your horse at the girth—you may use your outside leg slightly behind or in front of the girth if necessary. Your hands must be strongly fixed and pulled backwards of the normal position. You should use the neck rein or the direct and indirect reins, but your hand should be moved so that the reins are pressed against your horse's neck at, or just above, the withers. Do not haul your horse around with your hands: Use your legs and seat to drive him into the turn.

Your horse should continue to trot on all four legs throughout the turn. If he does not, increase the driving action of your legs. He should settle his weight (you should feel him do this) onto his haunches, and lightly trot around the haunches

Figure 7–71. Broken lines and broken lines with one-quarter turn on the haunches.

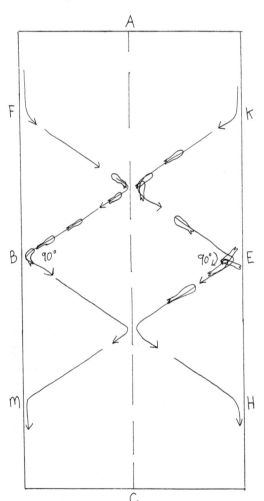

Figure 7–72. Chocolate is turning on her haunches to the right. Her hind legs are together, and she crosses her forelegs, with her left foreleg passing in front of her right foreleg. Her head is turned slightly in the direction of her movement. You can see the rider's aids—left leg behind the girth, left indirect and right direct reins, weight down in the saddle.

with his front end. His haunches should trot in place. You will need to practice quite a bit before you achieve perfection. Between the turns, your mount should move smoothly, without speeding or slowing his gait. He should move without wavering on the straight lines and turn without fighting your hands or legs. This will take plenty of practice for both you and your horse.

Common faults are as follows: The horse stops trotting on the rear (not enough leg pressure); he throws his head up or out (too much hand pressure, leg aids too light); the horse skids around on the rear end (not enough leg); he trots a small turn without doing a quarter-turn on the haunches (too light aids with hands, legs, and seat); he turns on the back more than on the front, thus doing a turn on the forehand (the aids are unco-ordinated).

A summary of aids for the broken lines with quarter-turn on the haunches follows (see Figure 7-73):

1. Prepare to turn by increasing tension in seat and reins.

2. Shift your weight backwards by dropping your weight into the saddle.

Figure 7-73. One-quarter turn on the haunches.

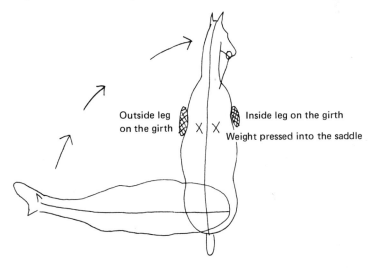

Outside leg on the girth

Inside leg on the girth

Weight pressed into the saddle

3. Press both legs into your horse at the girth.

4. Pull your hands backwards of the normal position.

5. Move both reins in the direction of the turn, and fix your hands.

6. Drive with your seat and legs. Use the crop on the outside, if necessary.

7. Keep your horse trotting. Do not sacrifice movement for a small turn. It is better to get a poor turn than to lose the trot.

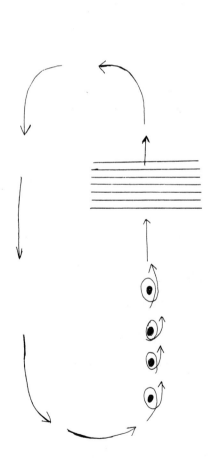

Figure 7–74. Cavaletti III: Place poles at least 20 feet from the cavaletti and about 20 feet apart. Ride at the walk and at the sitting trot.

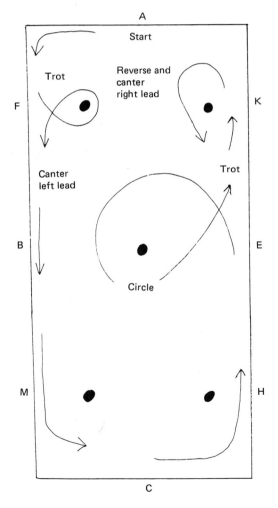

Figure 7–75. Pole bending VIII.

PRACTICE RIDE 8

Letter	*Movement*
A	Enter, walk. English riders on contact. Track up center line.
X	Halt. Stand to the count of five. Trot, posting.
C	Track left.
B	Large circle, width of the ring.
B	Continue trotting and posting.
C	Large circle, width of ring.
C	Sit the trot.
E	Figure eight.
E	Continue at sitting trot.
B	Figure eight.
B	Continue at sitting trot.
H	Small circle.
K	Small circle.
F	Small circle.
M	Half-circle.
F	Halt. Rein-back three steps. Walk on loose rein.

LESSON 14:
LEADS AT THE CANTER; JUMPING I

	Mount.	
	Review school figures (practice rides).	**15 minutes**
A /	**Leads at the canter.**	**30 minutes**
B /	**Beginning jumping—*or*—**	**15 minutes**
	Pole bending	
	Quick dismount.	

A / Leads at the Canter

By now you should be able to distinguish the canter leads. Hopefully, you can tell them by feel. If not, surely you can tell by looking at the shoulders and forelegs of your mount. Now you should learn to get the lead you desire.

Your horse should take the inside lead while cantering in the ring. If he is tracking to the right, he should be put on the right lead; if he is tracking left, he should be put on the left lead. Taking the correct lead will give him more stability on the turns. Horses have a great deal of difficulty cantering through corners on the incorrect lead. Usually they will change leads—perhaps only on the front—or drop to a fast trot.

It seems that every book on riding outlines a different method of obtaining the canter on a specific lead. Most of the methods are frankly incorrect, as they call for pushing the

Figure 7–76. Aids for the right lead.

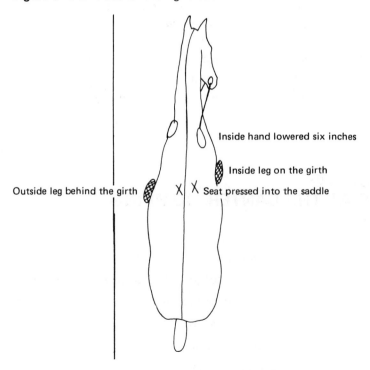

Inside hand lowered six inches

Inside leg on the girth

Outside leg behind the girth

Seat pressed into the saddle

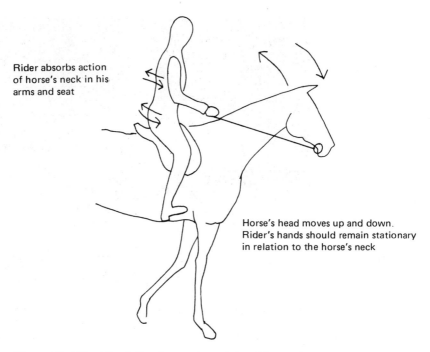

Rider absorbs action
of horse's neck in his
arms and seat

Horse's head moves up and down.
Rider's hands should remain stationary
in relation to the horse's neck

Figure 7–77. The following action of the rider at the canter.

horse's hind end off the track, or bending his neck to one side. These methods call for catching the horse off balance and throwing him into the desired lead. You should not use them, as they are poor horsemanship, and a sign of a mediocre rider.

If you have mastered Method 1, Lesson 11, using the half-halt, you should have little difficulty performing a correct canter depart on a specific lead. Follow these directions (see Figures 7-76 and 7-77):

1. Start from a slow trot with even strides. English horses should be on contact. (Later, you will learn to canter from a walk.)

2. Prepare to canter. After you straighten from a turn is a good time to start.

3. Lower your inside hand about six inches. For the right lead, lower your right hand; for the left lead, lower your left hand. Western riders should shift their rein hand to the right or left side of the withers.

4. Do a half-halt.

Figure 7–78a. Anrock is striking off into the canter on the right lead. You can see that he is pushing off his left hind leg. His leading foreleg is the last one to leave the ground. The rider is using her weight and legs to drive Anrock forward. She has her legs too far forward, making her seat insecure. Also, her weight is too far back in the saddle. Both of these problems are caused in part by her saddle—it is much too big for her. You should try to ride in a saddle that fits both your legs and your seat.

Figure 7–78b. Chocolate is in the process of beginning the canter on the right lead. Her rider apparently thinks she should be on the left lead, as she is leaning to the left and looking down. This is one of the most common and most serious mistakes in canter departs. You should not lean or look down. Both actions might put your horse into the canter on the wrong lead.

Figure 7–79. After the strike-off, Anrock continues on the right lead. His right foreleg seems to lead, since it reaches farther forward than his left hind leg.

5. Immediately drive your horse forward, and unfix your hands. You should drive with the inside leg on the girth, and the outside leg behind the girth. Your inside leg and the action of your seat pressing down into the saddle are the most important aids. Push your horse forward by pressing your seat bones into the saddle. If necessary, use the crop—either behind the girth on the outside, or on the inside shoulder.

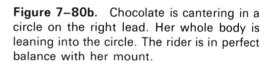

Figure 7–80a. Now Anrock is cantering on the left lead. His left foreleg seems to lead his body. However, he starts each stride with his right hind leg. His left foreleg is the last leg to hit the ground in the stride.

Figure 7–80b. Chocolate is cantering in a circle on the right lead. Her whole body is leaning into the circle. The rider is in perfect balance with her mount.

6. Check the leads. If he is on the wrong one, go to a slow trot and try again. Sometimes it might take several tries: All horses prefer one lead over the other. If your horse becomes upset, walk him until he relaxes, then try again.

You should be learning to ride the canter on contact (English) or without holding on to the mane (all riders). The horse moves his head and neck quite a bit while cantering. You must relax your arms and shoulders so that you can follow this action. Since your hands should remain at about the same spot with relation to your horse's neck, you can help yourself by resting one finger of each hand gently against the neck. Do not press very hard. Keep your fingers relaxed on the reins. Your back should be straight and fairly still: You should absorb the action of the canter with the small of your back, your seat, and your legs.

B / Beginning Jumping (optional)

Unless you ride huntseat and really want to learn to jump, skip this section. Always use a saddle and a hard hat when you jump. Never jump bareback or bare-headed. You may fall off and get hurt. Jumping can be fun, but it is always potentially very dangerous. You should never take chances. You should never jump unless someone is around to help you if you do fall from your mount.

It's a good idea to see how your horse reacts around jumps before you start. Set a few jumps in the ring along the track. Lay the rails on the ground. Your horse should walk and trot over the rails without jumping, and without excitement. If he acts upset, or tries to leap, you should not jump him without expert supervision. Get a quieter horse, or find a riding instructor who can help you by pointing out your mistakes and who is able to give you advice on how to handle your horse. Since he has gone quietly through the cavaletti, he will probably be quiet over the jumps. However, some horses have been whipped over big jumps, and they never seem to forget it.

Figure 7–81. Get your horse familiar with the jump before you try to take him over it. He should walk and trot over the rail without the least rushing or hesitation.

Figure 7–82. Both Chocolate and her rider show good form over this low jump. Chocolate is pushing off both her hind legs. The rider is in the correct position, well up on her horse's neck. The reins are loose, and her knees are against the saddle.

Now you are ready to begin learning to jump (for the sequence of action and the correct position, see Figures 7-83 and 7-84). Set one jump at the end of the cavaletti, nine or ten feet from the last cavaletti rail. Lay the jump rail on the ground. Practice with the rail on the ground until you feel comfortable. Then cross two rails in the jump so that the center of the jump is about 18 inches high. You will gradually raise the jump until it is about three feet in height. This process might take weeks. Don't push yourself. Take your time in learning to jump.

To jump with the cavaletti, follow these steps:

1. Approach the cavaletti as usual, at a walk. (Later, use the trot.) Aim for the center of the cavaletti, and hold your horse straight. He should be traveling with steady, even strides.

2. Ride through the cavaletti. Remain in the saddle so you can drive your horse with your seat. Keep him moving at an even pace without hesitation or speeding. Keep him in the center of the cavaletti, aimed at the center of the jump.

3. When you reach the end of the cavaletti, and your horse has stepped over the last rail, immediately take the jumping position. This is different than the rising position. You should come forward in the saddle and move your hands as far up your horse's neck as possible. Keep your legs in place. Do not pull your calves up against your mount. Flex forward from your knees.

4. Now, kick your mount with both heels. If the rail is raised at all, the kick should cause him to jump. If he doesn't jump, kick harder the next time. Do not pull your knees off the saddle when you kick.

5. You should not be thrown back into the saddle by the jump. You should remain in the jumping position until your horse lands—and he should continue at the walk or the trot, and not break into a gallop. To guard against falling back into the saddle, grab the horse's mane before the jump. After the jump, settle gently into the saddle, put your mount back on contact, and return to the cavaletti.

6. Learning to jump correctly will take time. Do not rush yourself or your mount. Your horse should remain calm at all times. If he gets at all upset, check to see if you are falling onto his back during or after the jump, or jerking his mouth with the reins at any time during the jump. Chances are that you are making one or both of the above mistakes. It is very easy to pretend that you are making no errors in your form, and that your horse is simply being stubborn. However,

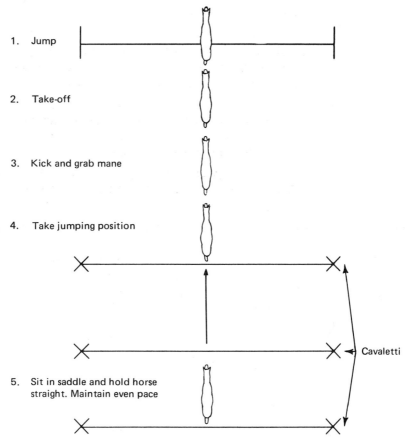

1. Jump

2. Take-off

3. Kick and grab mane

4. Take jumping position

Cavaletti

5. Sit in saddle and hold horse straight. Maintain even pace

Figure 7–83. Sequence of action of a jump.

Figure 7–84. The jumping position
1. Rider's weight is supported by knees and stirrups.
2. Hands are well up on the neck, allowing the horse free use of his head and neck.
3. Toes are in line with the knee.
4. Heels are down.
5. Back is straight, head is up.
6. Eyes look forward.
7. Knees are pressed well into saddle.
8. Toes are turned out at relaxed angle; they do not rotate outward on the jump.
9. Rider's seat is completely out of the saddle.

horses do not suddenly become difficult to jump for no reason. If your horse suddenly begins to misbehave, you should suspect that you are accidentally hurting him when he does jump.

Below is a summary of the sequence of action in jumping:

1. Ride through the cavaletti.

2. After your horse steps over the last rail, take the jumping position. Push your hands well up the horse's neck.

Figure 7–85. Cavaletti IV.

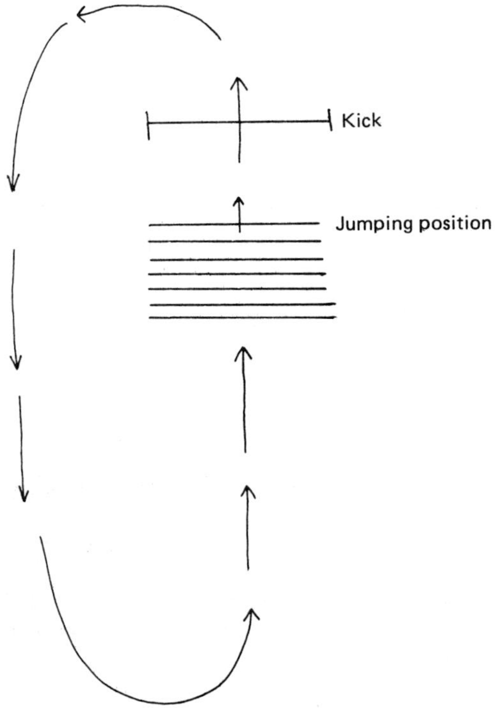

Figure 7–86. Pole bending IX.

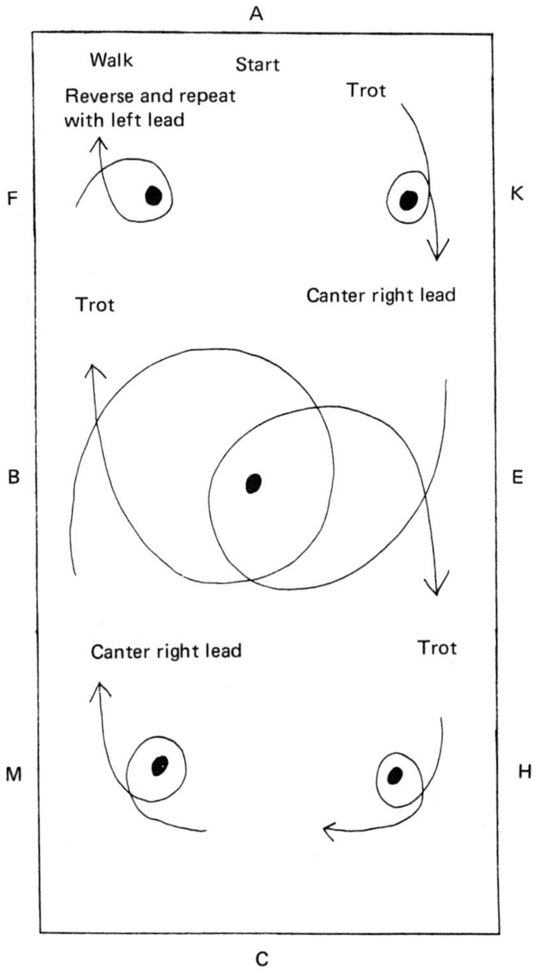

3. Kick your horse.

4. Hang on over the jump.

5. Remain out of the saddle for two strides after the jump.

6. Repeat.

LESSON 15:
CANTER DEPARTS FROM THE WALK; JUMPING II

	Mount.	
	Review school figures (practice rides).	**30 minutes**
A /	**Canter departs from the walk.**	**10 minutes**
B /	**Jumping—*or*—**	**20 minutes**
	Pole bending.	
	Dismount.	

A / Canter Departs from the Walk

Some horses prefer to canter from the walk, while others insist on trotting one or two strides first. Naturally, cantering from the walk will be much easier for you if your horse cooperates. If your horse is one of those that tries to trot before he canters, do not be upset. Simply ask him to canter from the walk everytime you canter. Sooner or later, your horse will probably learn to canter without trotting first.

To canter from the walk, follow this sequence:

1. Prepare to canter. Choose a letter as a place to start your canter.

2. At the letter, half-halt.

3. Release. At the same time, give the aids to canter (inside hand down, inside leg on the girth, outside leg behind the girth).

4. Push with your seat.

5. Follow the action of the horse with your hands and seat.

6. Do not lean forward or backwards. Do not try to whip your horse into the canter. If you use the aids correctly, you will get a canter. If you get a trot, go back to a walk and try again.

7. Check to be sure you are on the correct lead.

B / Jumping

Do not advance yourself in jumping until you can take a jump at the end of the cavaletti in fairly good form. You should be able to jump two feet from the walk and two-and-a-half feet from the trot. Once you can consistently jump these heights without losing your form, you can go on to the exercises described below.

FIRST EXERCISE

Place another jump with the cavaletti. This jump should be placed 18 feet (small horses and ponies) or 24 feet (horses 15.2 hands and over) behind the first jump. It must be lined up so that it is the same distance from the first jump at both ends. The height should be about the same as the height of the first jump. You will go through the cavaletti at a walk or trot, take the jumping position, and jump the first jump. Then you will return to the saddle and trot to the second jump. Hold your horse straight and aim towards the center of the second jump. Keep your thighs and the upper portion of your calves pressed into your mount to drive him into the jump without swerving or hesitation. About 10 feet before the jump, take the jumping position, and kick. As there is little space between the jumps, you must move fast. You will need a lot of practice to do this exercise correctly.

SECOND EXERCISE

Place four jumps in the ring (see Jumping I Figure 7-88). Practice taking the jumps at a walk and at a trot. The jumps should vary in height from 18 inches to 29 inches. If you are very brave, you may use a three foot jump. Always take the jumping

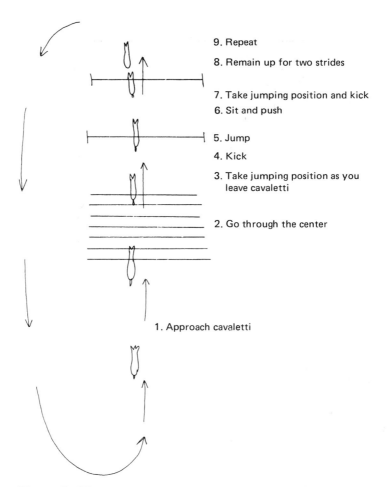

9. Repeat

8. Remain up for two strides

7. Take jumping position and kick
6. Sit and push

5. Jump

4. Kick

3. Take jumping position as you leave cavaletti

2. Go through the center

1. Approach cavaletti

Figure 7–87.   Cavaletti V.

position about 10 feet before the jump, and kick. Always ride into the center of the jump. Do not jump the sides of the jump, or the standards. Do not jump at any angle except 90 degrees to the rail.

Sequence for jumping without cavaletti:

1. Approach jump at a 90 degree angle to the center of the jump.
2. About 10 feet from jump, take the jumping position.
3. One stride later, kick.
4. Hang on.
5. Stay out of the saddle for two strides after the jump.

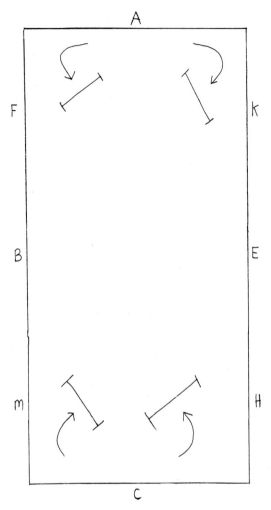

Figure 7–88. Jumping I.

PRACTICE RIDE 9

Letter	Movement
A	Begin at the trot. Track up the center line. English riders should post.
X	Halt. Stand five seconds. Trot. English riders post.
C	Track right.
M	Sit the trot.
B	Figure eight.
B	Continue at sitting trot.
A	Circle width of the ring.
E	Reverse across the mid-line.
B	Track left.
C	Circle width of the ring.
E	Figure eight.
E	Continue at sitting trot.
K	Walk.
F	Canter left lead.
F	Once around the ring. Walk.
B	Reverse across the mid-line.
E	Track right.
M	Canter, right lead. Go once around the ring.
M	Walk, loose rein.

LESSON 16:
LEAD CHANGES; EXTENDED GAITS; JUMPING III

Mount.

Review (practice rides).   **30 minutes**

A / **Simple lead changes.**   **15 minutes**

B / **Extended gaits.**   **15 minutes**

    Quick dismount from canter (optional).

    Optional jumping

C / **Jumping at the canter.**

    Jumping courses.

A / Simple Lead Changes

Whenever you change direction at the canter (for example, on a half-circle), you should change leads. Otherwise, your horse will be cantering on the wrong lead when he returns to the track, and will probably skid on the next corner. Two ways to change lead exist. These are the simple lead change, and the flying lead change. The flying lead change is done without dropping from the canter. A correct flying lead change is difficult, and part of advanced riding. Therefore, it is beyond the scope of this manual.

A simple lead change is a change done by temporarily putting the horse into a trot or a walk. Simple lead changes are also difficult on all but well schooled horses. Other animals tend to get upset and begin to rush and pull. You should practice only a few simple lead changes at a time if your horse becomes at all upset. Do not push him, as he will become more frantic with time. It is better to do one simple lead change a day, and keep your horse calm, than to do seven and bring an upset, sweating animal back to the stable.

You may practice lead changes on the diagonal, the half-circle, or the reverse across the ring (see Figures 7–92 and 7–93). On most horses, the change on the diagonal is easiest, as you have more room.

Canter your horse on, for example, the right lead. You might canter a circle the width of the ring at B to help relax him. Be careful that he doesn't skid as he turns. Hold him steady with your legs and don't let him range his haunches out of the circle. Then, return to the track, and canter to K. Turn onto the diagonal, again guarding against skids with your seat and legs. As

Figure 7-89. The rider is bringing Anrock from a canter on the right lead to a trot for the simple lead change. He has already broken his canter. In one more stride he will be trotting.

Figure 7-90. Now Anrock is trotting. His rider seems to be having a little trouble, as she is behind in these pictures. This lead change is being done on the track for the convenience of the photographer. You should practice lead changes on the diagonal or on half-circles.

you approach X, apply fixed hands and drop your weight to slow your mount to a walk or a trot. Steady his gait—he should trot slowly, or walk evenly. After three, five, or nine strides (learn to count them), ask for the canter depart on the left lead. Return to the track at K, being careful to canter through the corner. At E, circle the width of the ring to relax your mount. Then walk on a loose rein.

Figure 7-91. Anrock is now cantering on his left lead after a successful simple lead change. Notice that he has changed leads on a straight line with a straight body. You should avoid bending your horse when you change leads.

Some horses prefer to canter from the walk. Others prefer to depart from the trot, or refuse to drop from the canter to the walk in a short distance. You should plan your practice of the above exercise accordingly. Ideally, you should have as few strides of the walk or trot as possible. Do not, however, push your horse. He should be relaxed when you ask for the canter depart. If he is tense or rushing his strides, let him go a while longer before you ask. If he anticipates the lead change, make him trot from X several times without asking for the canter.

When you change lead on the half-circle, straighten your horse out of the semi-circle and ask on the line to the track. On

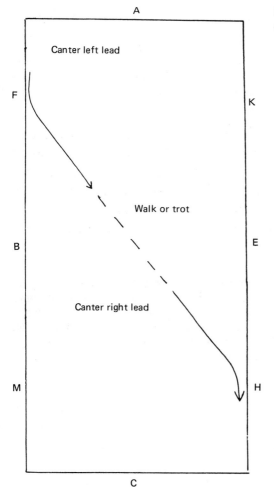

Figure 7–92. Simple lead changes on the diagonal.

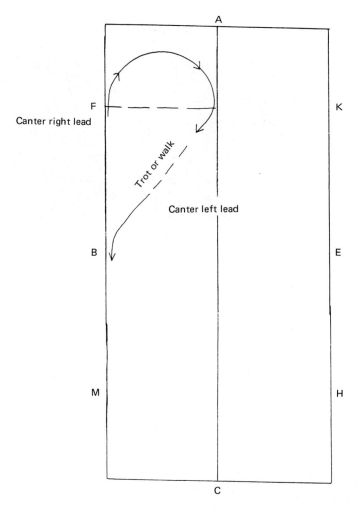

Figure 7–93. Simple lead changes on the half-circle.

the reverse through the ring, straighten your horse after turning into the ring. Then drop to the walk or trot and ask for the lead change.

B / Extended Gaits

When your horse does a true extended gait, he will take longer strides, but will not speed the rhythm of his gait. The gait will become faster but the number of beats per minute will remain

Figure 7–94. Chocolate does a nice extended trot. She is bringing her legs both upward and forward and is really using herself.

the same. To obtain an extended gait (walk, trot, or canter) follow these steps. (Refer also to Figures 7-99a, b, c, and d):

1. Fix your hands (but let your horse extend his neck).

2. At the same time, increase the action of your legs. Push with your thighs and calves.

3. Push with your seat.

4. Do not lean forward or backwards.

Figure 7–95. Anrock has longer legs than Chocolate. He shows less extension for his size than she does for her size. His rider should not be leaning backward.

Figure 7–96. Chocolate is traveling at the extended canter. Her head is up, and her legs are extending forward. The extended canter is practiced in the ring. You should sit in the saddle at this gait.

Figure 7–97. Now Chocolate is galloping. You should gallop only in fields where you have plenty of room. The rider is in the correct galloping position—forward, with her hands down on Chocolate's neck. You can tell how much faster Chocolate is moving now than she was at the extended canter. Western riders should also stand up and lean forward at the gallop. The gallop is a rather dangerous gait for both you and your horse. You should not practice it too often.

5. If your horse speeds his rhythm, or breaks into another gait, slow him and try again.

6. Always practice for short distances on a straight line. Do not tire your horse. Do not extend on the turns.

7. Do not jump from the extended walk or trot. You may jump from an extended canter.

People frequently jump from the hand-gallop. The hand-gallop is a controlled gallop that is more extended and has a faster rhythm than a canter. The horse will extend his head and neck, and carry his center of balance to the front. To stay with him, you must take the galloping position (see Figure 7-98). Lean forward, carrying your weight into your knees and the stirrups. Place your hands against your horses's neck. Since English riders ride the gallop on strong contact, it is called a hand-gallop (from gallop in hand). Western riders should also stand in the saddle and shorten the reins at the gallop.

Figure 7–98. The galloping position

You should push your weight into your knees and stirrups, and place your hands on the sides of your horse's neck. When you wish to slow your mount, you should return to the saddle so you can use your legs and seat. The speed of the hand-gallop is about 18 miles per hour. At no time should you push your mount into a fast gallop or a full run. Running horses are more likely to injure themselves. In fact, almost all injuries to the horse occur during the gallop and the run.

Practice the hand-gallop after your mount has warmed up at slower gaits. You should not gallop in the ring, which is too small, or in a large, open area—this is too dangerous, since he might run away with you. Choose a small, enclosed field without trees, and free of other horses. Stop galloping before your horse becomes winded or lathered. Always walk him for about fifteen minutes after you gallop.

Never race with other horses. If you want to race, become a jockey. Racing pleasure horses is dangerous to both horse and rider.

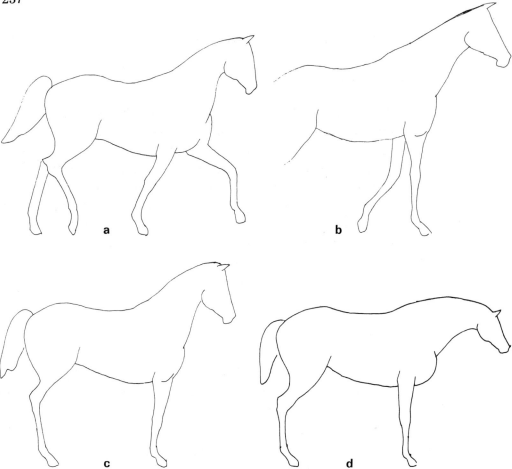

Figure 7–99a. The center of balance shifts as the horse changes speed and extension. At the school gaits, the horse is balanced on a line through his back. The rider should carry his weight over the horse's back to be in balance with his mount.

Figure 7–99b. As the horse increases his speed, his center of balance shifts toward his withers. The rider must lean forward to remain with his horse at speed.

Figure 7–99c. At the halt, the horse should be balanced over all four legs. His center of balance is slightly to the rear of its position while he is in motion. When he reins back, the horse will shift his center of balance even farther to the rear. The rider stays with the horse by weighting his seat (pressing the points of his buttocks into the saddle).

Figure 7–99d. An untrained horse will move heavily on the front. His center of balance is over his front legs. His head is low, and he drags his hind legs. A horse that pulls will also weight his front. The rider should sit slightly behind the horse's center of balance and encourage the horse to raise his head through active use of the rider's legs and seat. Do not pull up on the reins.

C / Jumping at the Canter and Jumping Courses

JUMPING AT THE CANTER

Jumping II is an exercise in jumping from the canter (see Figures 7–103 and 7–104). You should have your mount traveling in a smooth, even canter on the correct lead. Sit in the saddle until you are about 10 feet from the jump. Then come into the jumping position and jump as before. Always sit in the saddle between jumps when jumping from the canter. If you jump from the hand-gallop (do this on the jump course or cross country only—never gallop in the little ring), you will remain in the galloping position between jumps, except on sharp turns. Then you will sit to give you more control as you drive your mount around the turn.

JUMPING COURSES

Once you are beginning to feel at ease with jumping from a walk, a trot, and a canter, you can learn to jump courses. Set up several jumps in a small, enclosed field. These jumps should be about 29–36 inches in height. If you have a large horse and

Figure 7–100. After you have learned to jump with the cavaletti, you can start taking small fences in the ring or in the field. Start with a single jump and gradually build your course until you are taking eight or nine fences in a row. Always be sure to take the correct jumping position. Don't get left behind.

Figure 7–101. When you are going over one jump, you should have your head up, looking toward the next obstacle. A rail laid on the ground under the jump helps your mount judge his take-off. You can set up some jumps with the ground rail and some without. The rider is cantering Chocolate over a small course (2-foot jumps) and being watched intently by Boobie, the dog.

plenty of nerve, you may set some jumps 42–48 inches high. Do not set any of the jumps over 48 inches, or four feet, in height.

You may combine two jumps to make a spread or set several jumps in a series for an in-and-out (two jumps in a row, 24 or 48 feet apart) or a triple (three jumps in a row, each 24 or 48 feet apart). (Earlier I discussed jumping two jumps at the end of the cavaletti: the method of jumping is essentially the same for an in-and-out or a triple.) Always be careful to space your jumps correctly, so that they will not be dangerous traps for your horse. You may make other jumps if you desire. A pattern is included in Figure 7-102 for several different types of jumps.

The first time you jump a course, walk your horse until you are 20 feet from the jump. Then take the jumping position, and trot him over. After he has taken all the jumps, you may begin trotting the course. With some practice at the trot, you will be ready to canter. Do not canter the course unless you are very secure in the saddle at the canter, and unless you can easily canter jumps in the ring.

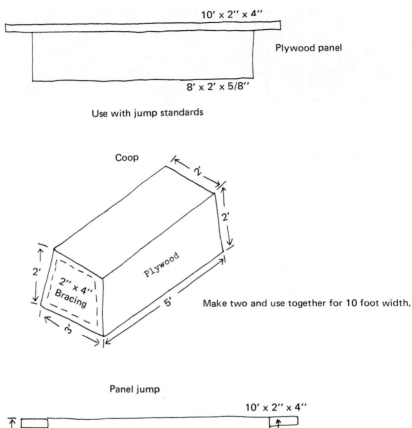

10' x 2" x 4"

Plywood panel

8' x 2' x 5/8"

Use with jump standards

Coop

2'

2'

2" x 4" Bracing

Plywood

5'

3'

Make two and use together for 10 foot width.

Panel jump

10' x 2" x 4"

1'

Plywood panel

2'

8' x 2'-1' x 5/8"

Use with jump standards

Figure 7–102. Panel jump.

Always ride towards the jumps at 90 degrees from the center of the jump. Keep your legs against your mount from the upper calves through your seat, and drive him straight into the jump. Be careful not to jerk his mouth or bang his back as you ride over, and do not return to the saddle until he has landed on the other side. Never jump without a saddle and a hard hat, and never jump unless someone is around who can, if necessary, help you. Don't take chances, and you will have good, safe fun.

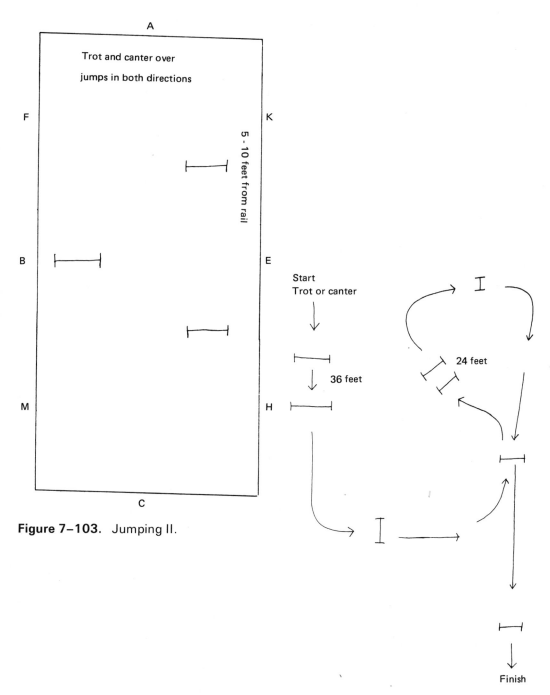

Figure 7–103. Jumping II.

Figure 7–104. Sample jump course.

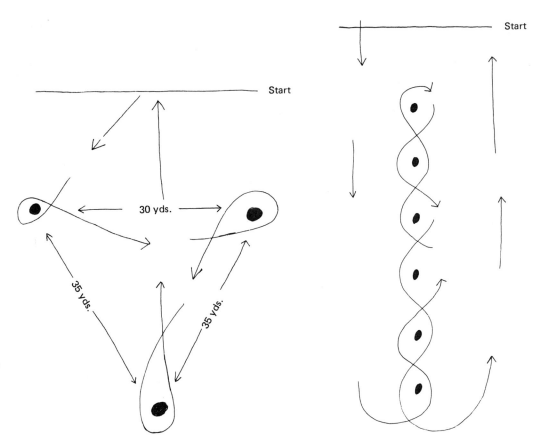

Figure 7–105. Pole bending X: use barrels instead of poles. Do at the walk, trot, canter, and gallop. This is called "Barrel Racing."

Figure 7–106. Pole bending XI; place the poles 20 feet apart. Do at the walk, trot, canter, and gallop. Change diagonals or leads each time you change direction.

TEST YOUR FORM: WESTERN

For best results, have a friend snap several pictures of you while you ride. Then compare the pictures to the drawing in Figure 6-26. Answer the questions below.

1. Are your arms in a straight line with your body?
2. Are you sitting straight in the saddle?
3. Are your toes even with, or just slightly in front of, your knees?
4. Are your heels lower than your toes?
5. Are you close to the saddle at all times?
6. Do you look comfortable and relaxed?

TEST YOUR FORM: ENGLISH

For best results, have a friend snap several pictures of you while you ride. Compare the pictures with the drawing in Figure 6-25. Then answer the questions below.

1. Are your hands over, and slightly in front of, your horse's withers?
2. Is your body vertical, except when posting? Is your back straight?
3. Are your heels down at all times? Do your toes turn at a relaxed angle?
4. Is there a straight line from your knee through your toes?
5. Is there a straight line from your elbow to the bit?
6. Are your eyes up and your shoulders back?
7. Do you look comfortable and relaxed?
8. Is there a straight line from your elbow to the bit?

9. Are your hands well down the horse's neck?

10. Is there a straight line from your knee to your toes?

11. Are your heels down at all times? Do your toes turn at a relaxed angle?

12. Is your seat out of the saddle?

13. Are your eyes up and your shoulders back?

14. Is your back straight?

15. Is there a straight line from your knee to your toes? Are your toes turned out at a relaxed angle?

16. Are your hands pushed well up your horse's neck? Are the reins slack?

17. Is your seat out of the saddle?

18. Are your eyes up and your shoulders back?

19. Are your heels down at all times?

CHECK YOUR PROGRESS

Skill	Date
Smooth halt from a trot.	_____
Smooth trot from a halt.	_____
Broken lines without skidding.	_____
Quarter-turn on haunches at trot.	_____
Small circle without skidding.	_____
Figure eight with equal circles.	_____
Right lead at canter.	_____
Left lead at canter.	_____
Jump at end of cavaletti in good form.	_____
Canter depart on right lead from walk.	_____
Canter depart on left lead from walk.	_____
Jumping without cavaletti	_____
Lead change from right to left on diagonal.	_____
Lead change from left to right on diagonal.	_____

Lead change on half-circle.	_____
Extended walk.	_____
Extended trot.	_____
Hand-gallop.	_____
Jumping from canter.	_____
Jumping courses.	_____
Quick dismount from canter.	_____

FINAL EXAM

Included are four riding tests. Memorize the tests, or have a friend call them as you ride. You should be able to ride each test smoothly, without fault.

Riding Test 1

Letter	Movement
A	Enter ring at trot. English riders post. Go up center line.
X	Halt. Continue at trot. English riders post.
C	Track left.
M	Sit the trot.
C	Circle left, width of the ring.
C	Canter on left lead. Circle left width of the ring.
C	Continue on track at the canter.
A	Trot. English riders post.
H–X–F	Trot the diagonal. English riders change posting diagonals at X.
F	Sit the trot.
C	Circle right the width of the ring.
C	Canter, right lead. Circle the width of the ring.
C	Continue on the track.
E	Trot, sitting.
B	Walk, loose rein.

Riding Test 2

Letter	Movement
A	Enter ring at sitting trot. Go up center line.
X	Halt. Count to five. Proceed at the sitting trot.
C	Track left.
H–X–F	Ride the diagonal
K–X–M	Ride the diagonal.
H	Small circle.
K	Half-circle to E.
H	Half-circle to E.
A–F	Between A and F pick up the canter, left lead.
E	Circle the width of the ring.
A	Trot, sitting.
H–X–F	Extend the trot.
E	Walk.
B	Trot, sitting.
A–K	Pick up the canter, right lead.
B	Circle the width of the ring.
A	Trot, sitting.
E	Halt. Rein-back three steps. Walk on a loose rein.

Riding Test 3

Letter	Movement
A	Enter ring at the walk. Track up the center line.
X	Halt. Count to five. Trot, sitting.
C	Track right.
B	Figure-eight.
F	Half-circle to B.
H	Small circle.
F	Broken lines with square turns.
H	Broken lines with quarter-turns on the haunches.
A	Walk.

B	Halt. Half-turn on forehand.
B	Walk.
A	Halt. Half-turn on forehand.
A	Walk.
B	Canter on left lead, once around the ring.
B	Gradually go to walk, through the trot. Walk on loose reins.
E	Reverse through the mid-line. At B track right. English riders go onto contact with the reins.
A	Canter on right lead.
B	Gradually go to walk, through the trot. Walk on loose reins.

Riding Test 4

Letter	Movement
A	Enter the ring at sitting trot. Go up the center line.
X	Halt. Rein-back three steps. Proceed at sitting trot.
C	Track left.
F–X–H	Change diagonals, extended trot.
B	Walk.
K	Canter right lead.
B	Circle width of the ring. Continue on the track at canter.
K–X–M	Ride the diagonal. At X, trot, and pick up the canter again on the left lead.
M	Continue to canter on the track, left lead.
E	Gradually come to the walk through the trot. Walk on loose reins.
F	English riders go onto contact.
B	Canter left lead.
E	Circle width of the ring. Continue on the track at canter.
F–X–H	Ride the diagonal. At X, trot, and pick up the canter on the right lead.

H	Continue on track at the canter.
B	Trot, sitting.
A	Turn up the center line.
X	Halt. Count to five. Proceed on a loose rein at the walk.

Written Tests (100 points possible; passing score, 75)

1. True or false (1 point each):

    a. Whenever you change direction at the canter, you should change leads.

    b. The flying lead change is done through the trot.

    c. Simple lead changes are very easy.

    d. Lead changes may be done on the diagonal or half-circle.

    e. On a simple lead change you should walk thirteen steps.

    f. When you change on the half-circle, change during the semi-circle.

    g. When your horse does an extended gait, he will speed the rhythm of his strides.

    h. Never jump from the extended canter.

    i. Never gallop your horse.

    j. To trot from the halt, hit your horse with the crop three times.

    k. Small circles are circles with a diameter half the width of the ring.

    l. Figure eights are two small circles strung together.

    m. You should ride figure eights at A and C.

    n. Broken lines are serpentines with square turns.

    o. You should do the quarter-turn on the haunches at the halt.

    p. Your horse should pivot around his outside hind leg on the quarter-turn on the haunches.

q. You should be able to tell the canter leads without looking.

r. To put your horse on the right lead, pull his head to the left.

s. To put your horse on the right lead, pull his head to the right.

t. At the canter, your hands should move up and down on the horse's neck.

u. In the jumping position, your hands should be well up your horse's neck.

v. Always keep your heels down.

w. Jumping is very easy and can be done bareback.

x. Your horse should remain calm at all times.

y. A good rider never loses his temper.

2. Multiple choice (1 point each):

a. When your horse trots
   (1) he nods his head.
   (2) his head remains absolutely still.
   (3) he raises his head, then nods.

b. Riding bareback
   (1) is dangerous.
   (2) is valuable only for children.
   (3) is excellent for building nerve and balance.

c. A crop is
   (1) the rear end of the horse.
   (2) a short whip.
   (3) a type of boot.

d. Western riders
   (1) hold the reins in one hand.
   (2) hold the reins in the left hand.
   (3) hold the reins in the right hand.

e. A Western bit
   (1) is very mild.
   (2) is severe.

        (3) can be used like a snaffle.

  f. Leg action can be

        (1) behind the girth.
        (2) very severe.
        (3) too fast.

  g. Any horse can be trained

        (1) to eat apples.
        (2) to be a race horse.
        (3) to neck rein.

  h. To ride on contact

        (1) remove the saddle.
        (2) shorten the reins.
        (3) stiffen your wrists.

  i. Hands may be

        (1) good, quiet, poor, or pulling.
        (2) good, quiet, poor, or rich.
        (3) good, bad, quiet or noisy.

  j. When you use the right direct rein, your horse will

        (1) stop.
        (2) turn left.
        (3) turn right.

  k. When you use the right indirect rein, your horse will

        (1) stop.
        (2) turn left.
        (3) turn right.

  l. When you use the right direct and the left indirect rein, your horse will

        (1) stop.
        (2) turn left.
        (3) turn right.

  m. When you use the right direct rein and the left direct rein, your horse will

(1) stop.

(2) turn left

(3) turn right.

n.   To turn right, you should

(1) use the outside leg on the girth.

(2) use the inside leg on the girth.

(3) use the inside leg behind the girth.

o.   To turn left, you should

(1) lean left.

(2) lean right.

(3) remain balanced in the saddle.

p.   You may circle the width of the ring at

(1) any point in the ring.

(2) letters A,B,C,D.

(3) letters A,B,C,E.

q.   A diagonal in the ring

(1) goes from corner to corner.

(2) goes from B to K.

(3) goes from K to M.

r.   Bending poles

(1) are an aid in teaching turns.

(2) are for children only.

(3) should be used only by Western riders.

s.   Double reins consist of

(1) upper curb and bottom snaffle.

(2) upper snaffle and lower curb.

(3) split reins.

t.   To halt

(1) pull back on the reins.

(2) fix your hands and push with your seat.

(3) lean backwards.

u.   In a half-turn on the forehand to the right

(1) the horse moves his haunches right.

        (2) he moves his haunches left.

        (3) he moves his forehand right.

  v. Half-circles

        (1) are performed at all letters.

        (2) are performed only at letters A and E.

        (3) are performed at all but A and C.

  w. A reverse across the mid-line

        (1) is from letters A to C.

        (2) is from letter B to E.

        (3) is anywhere in the ring.

  x. In a good square turn

        (1) haunches follow shoulders.

        (2) haunches move outside of the shoulders.

        (3) the horse stops and turns on his haunches.

  y. In using the cavaletti

        (1) ride only at the walk.

        (2) approach from 10 feet.

        (3) approach from 20 feet.

3. Define the following terms completely (1 point each):

a. Pommel	n. To ride a straight line
b. Leading rein	o. Change of hand
c. Crop	p. The rider's aids
d. Leg behind the girth	q. Period of suspension
e. Neck rein	r. Vibrating the reins
f. Skidding	s. Haunches
g. On contact	t. To range the haunches
h. Good hands	u. Following action of rider
i. Direct rein	v. School figures
j. Indirect rein	w. Canter depart
k. Curb	x. Simple lead change
l. Fixed hands	y. Hand-gallop
m. Pivot leg	

IV

IN
THE
OPEN

This section is a brief discussion of problems you may encounter with your mount during your lessons. If you chose a lesson horse wisely, as described in Part II, you should have few difficulties. However, no horse is perfect. If you ride for any length of time, you are sure to run into problems eventually. Chapter 8 helps you to be prepared when difficulties arise.

8 Problems with Your Horse in the Open

This part of the book deals with problems you may have while you are riding. Each problem is discussed individually, with causes, prevention, cures, and emergency procedures.

Horses sometimes develop vices, or incurably bad habits. These vices are fixed problems which even expert horsemen cannot always correct. For example, bucking can be a vice which renders a horse unsuitable for riding. Rearing can be a dangerous vice, as can bolting and running away. However, in this chapter, bucking, rearing, running, and other problems are treated as misbehaviors which are not fixed in the horse's mentality. Any horse may rear if the rider pulls too much on its mouth; and any horse may buck if the rider pounds upon its back with his seat.

I assume you have avoided riding a horse that has a serious vice. Any problems you may have, therefore, are probably caused by rider mistakes, misunderstandings between horse and rider, or by sudden, unpredictable circumstances. This chapter will help you deal with these aggravations and emergencies.

SHYING

Any horse may shy; and some horses "spook" much easier than others. When a horse shies or spooks, he raises his head suddenly in alarm and becomes tense all over. Then, he will either jump to one side, or bolt forward. His ears will be forward and he will snort and blow from his nostrils. Sometimes the horse will give warning by becoming tense and anxious for a while before he shies. At other times, the horse will leap suddenly sideways with no warning at all.

Shying is caused by fear. In the wild, horses are herd animals. They eat grass in large groups. Each member of the herd is alert for danger, such as snakes and predators. If a horse sees or smells danger—a wolf, a strange object, or even an unexpected rustle in the grass—he will start and snort, thus warning the rest of the herd so that they can gallop away. This instinct to shy and run has remained in the horse long after the need for it has passed. If your horse sees a strange object or a sudden movement (he's not likely to see a predator), he will act according to his instinct. He will experience sudden blind terror and a strong desire to flee.

A well-trained horse trusts his rider. After the initial fear response, the horse will calm and move on quietly. Also, after a horse has become accustomed to a trail, the objects on it will no longer seem strange or frightening to him. With patient training, any horse can become accustomed to anything.

You cannot prevent all shying, though you can take measures to decrease the frequency of sudden terror to your horse. If you are riding on strange trails, you can ride with other horses that are already accustomed to the area. When your horse becomes tense and nervous, you can calm him by patting his neck and speaking softly. Above all, you should never show fear when you are mounted. If your horse becomes tense, you must not become so afraid of his shying that you let your legs go limp. You can stop the horse briefly if you desire. Then drive him forward strongly with your legs, and hold firm contact with his mouth. If the horse is moving forward strongly against the bit, he is unlikely to shy or bolt suddenly.

Since you should put your horse on this strong contact only when he becomes tense and upset, you will not be able to prevent all shying. Many times, the horse will shy without warning. When this happens, your first concern will be to keep your seat. Don't be afraid to grab the saddle or the mane. If you become badly unseated, do an emergency dismount. You will find that if you develop a good seat—good form, strong legs, a flexible back—you will rarely become unseated when your mount shies.

When your seat is secure, you should gather the reins. If your horse bolts or behaves badly in any other manner, you must cope as described in later sections. Most horses will stand or walk on calmly if you pat their necks and talk in soothing tones. You should drive them forward with your legs.

Sometimes horses spook at an object by the side of the trail. If this happens, let the horse look at the object. If possible, let him smell it. Convince the horse that he has nothing to fear. Then, move on down the trail. You may dismount and lead your horse past the frightening object if you must.

NEVER WHIP A HORSE FOR SHYING!! Remember, the horse is reacting out of fear. Whipping him will merely reinforce his terror. Not being very bright, the horse will assume he has been whipped by the object of his fear. You make him more afraid by whipping him, and thus more likely to panic the next time he shies. A few good beatings can turn a quiet horse into a confirmed shier.

BOLTING

When a horse bolts, he leaps forward suddenly and stretches into a full gallop. Many horses never bolt; others bolt frequently. They may or may not run away, depending upon the reaction of the rider.

Usually, horses bolt because they are afraid. They may shy and bolt, or they may simply bolt forward away from the strange, frightening object. Young horses are particularly prone to this behavior. Other horses may bolt in an attempt to get their own way. Sometimes they will bolt and run to the pasture or barn. Or they may bolt in order to try to catch up with other horses on the trail.

To prevent bolting, follow the same procedure I recommended to prevent shying. When your horse acts upset, push him forward on contact. Western riders should also use contact on the reins under these circumstances. The general rule is: "To keep the horse under control, keep him moving on contact."

If your horse does bolt forward, immediately give strong aids for the halt. Drop your weight into the saddle and fix your hands. Applied soon enough, these aids will keep your mount from running away with you. If he catches you completely by surprise, he may be into a full gallop before you have collected the reins and secured your seat. Then you must deal with him as a runaway.

Never whip a horse for bolting. Make him halt briefly, then walk. Steady him with your hands and voice. It's a good idea to let him approach the object of his fear, if possible. You may dismount and lead him past the spot where he bolted, if you are unable to control him while you are mounted. Remember, bolting is usually caused by fear. Whipping the horse will reinforce his fear, and make him bolt faster the next time.

If you are certain that your horse bolted out of stubbornness, in an attempt to return to the pasture or to run after other horses, your reactions should be slightly different than those described above. Make him stop. Then walk on. Everytime your horse attempts to pull and move faster than you desire, halt. Make him stand until he is calm, then proceed at a walk. If he gives you too much grief, you might turn and make him walk away from the barn or the other horses. Whipping the horse will have little effect; however, a blow with the crop behind the girth will encourage him to walk in the direction you desire. Remember, do not pull upon his mouth. If you put your horse on strong contact, you must apply your legs equally as strong. Keep him moving forward. If the horse should begin to back up or rear, you must immediately move him forward.

RUNNING AWAY

Most horses run away as a result of bolting with fear. Some horses will run to the barn, or run to keep up with other horses. Sometimes runaways are caused by misunderstandings between horse and rider. The rider, without realizing it, gives the horse the aids for a fast gallop. Once the horse is running, the rider panics, and is thus unable to stop him.

With the use of good sense, you can prevent most runaways. Be on your guard when you ride past strange objects that might frighten your mount. Never race with other horses; and do not gallop in open spaces until you feel perfectly at ease at fast speeds.

Following are three procedures you may use to stop a runaway horse. The first two are easier on the horse, but might not work on all horses. Do not try these methods at all unless you have plenty of room, and are not headed rapidly towards woods or a busy highway. The last method will always work, but is very severe on the horse.

1. Drop your weight into the saddle and fix your hands strongly upon the reins. Hold this position. If the horse responds at all, he will begin to slow after a few strides. This method will not work if the horse gets badly above (head up) or behind (chin tucked to his chest) the bit, or if he is running with his head turned to one side.

2. Using the leading rein, turn the horse into a large circle. Keep him turning as you gradually reduce the size of the circle. This method will not work if you are in restrictive space, or if the horse merely turns his head to one side, and refuses to turn his body.

3. Use the pulley rein. This is a way of using the reins that is very effective in stopping any horse. The horse is pulled off balance, and must stop or fall. As mentioned before, the pulley rein is very severe. You should use it only when absolutely necessary.

To use the pulley rein, you must have one rein in each hand. Both reins must be fairly short. Place your left hand, with the rein, upon your horse's neck and grab the mane. Pull the other hand up sharply towards your chest. You are attempting to jerk your horse's head suddenly back to one side. If your horse merely turns his head, your

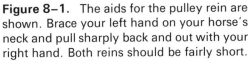

Figure 8–1. The aids for the pulley rein are shown. Brace your left hand on your horse's neck and pull sharply back and out with your right hand. Both reins should be fairly short.

Figure 8–2. The pulley rein will stop even a runaway very quickly. It is very severe and should not be used unless necessary. Chocolate is being stopped from a gallop in this picture. You can see from her open mouth and tossed head that she doesn't like the pulley rein one bit.

left rein is too long. If the horse does not turn his head, your right rein is too long. In both cases, shorten the reins, and try again.

Do not whip your horse for running away. Whipping will not correct the problem.

BARN SOUR

A barn sour horse tries to return to the stable, or refuses to leave his barn. Horses may also be sour about a pasture, or any other place where they are housed and fed. Usually other horses in the barn or pasture aggravate the problem by neighing and calling whenever they see the barn sour horse.

This problem is caused by a combination of the horse's natural desire to remain in familiar surroundings, and by rider mistakes. A weak rider will let the horse carry him to the barn. A foolish rider will gallop the last half mile home. The barn sour horse is aggravating and can be dangerous; however, unless the problem has become a set habit, it can be cured with persistence on your part.

If your horse refuses to leave the barn, turn him so that he is headed away from the barn, and whip him with the crop behind the girth. Put him on contact, and continue to drive him until he moves away from the barn. You may need to turn him away from the barn several times before he will yield to your demands. Use your heels, and apply the crop behind the girth on the outside to make him turn.

If your mount tries to carry you back to the barn, or if he speeds his gait when heading towards the barn, you should turn him away and make him walk away from the barn. If the horse tries to jog or run, you may stop him and make him stand immobile for a minute. Do not allow the horse to return to the barn until he is walking calmly on a loose rein. It will help if you make a practice of dismounting away from the barn and leading your horse to the stable.

Never run to the barn. Always walk your mount the last half-mile to the stable. This action brings him in cool, and helps to prevent the development of barn sour behavior.

REARING

When a horse rears, he stands upon his hind legs, and draws his forelegs up into the air. Some horses rear out of stubborness, and stallions rear when excited. However, most rearing is caused by poor biting and by rider mistakes.

A rearing horse is carrying all his weight over his hind legs.

He has no forward motion. A severe curb bit may make a horse displace his weight backwards over his hind legs and rear. Heavy hands will have the same effect, especially when combined with a weak seat and weak legs. The horse is caused to move his weight backwards by the lack of driving aids (making him move forward) and by the severity of the restraining aids (stopping forward movement). If the rider continues to pull upon the reins while the horse is rearing, he may pull the animal over backwards.

If your horse rears frequently, check your bit. Perhaps you should go to a milder one. Also, try to develop your seat, legs, and hands so that you ride the horse forward and do not cause him to displace his weight backwards. Your legs and seat should drive. The reins should merely guide and, when you wish to slow or halt, restrain. At no time should you pull upon the reins.

To stay with a rearing horse, let the reins loose. Lean forward as the horse goes up. You may wrap your arms around his neck if necessary. Do not lean backwards or hold yourself up with the reins. You might cause the horse to fall over on top of you. As soon as the horse touches his forefeet to the ground, hit him with the crop behind the girth. Hit him hard and keep at it until he moves forward. Be prepared, for the horse might bolt. However, you must give him a loose rein as you whip him. If you hold the horse on a tight rein, he will simply rear again. Usually one experience of this nature will cure the horse of rearing.

Several so-called cures are popular in certain circles. These cures may actually stop rearing, but they are dangerous to both horse and rider. Also, they do not treat the real cause of rearing—lack of forward motion. You should never do either of the following: pull your horse over backwards; or hit him between the ears with a board, bottle, or whip.

Also, never teach a horse to rear on command. This may be a showy trick; however, it is hard on the horse's hind legs, and can cause problems with your horse in other areas. As a general rule, you should never teach a riding horse tricks of any kind. If you want a trick horse, buy one especially for this kind of training.

BACKING

Sometimes you will come across a horse that begins to walk backwards when he is placed under stress. Maybe he is frightened by some object in the road, or perhaps he knows he has been disobedient in the ring. Green horses will sometimes back away from a strange object; however, the cause of this habit is usually poor training. Some riders use the deplorable practice of reining-back their mounts when the animals misbehave. Thus the horse learns to back under stress. The general rule in all riding should be: Always move your horse forward. Even when reining-back as a ring exercise, you should obtain the backward movement by pushing your horse forward into a fixed rein. As long as your horse is moving forward, you are at least potentially in control. When the horse begins to back, you lose control and become a helpless passenger. Never rein-back other than a few steps at a time. Never whip a horse backwards, and never allow a horse to move other than forwards when he is whipped. Never use reining-back as a punishment.

If your horse does begin moving backwards against your commands, you must make him go forward. Turning him in circles, dismounting, or merely halting his backward motion will not solve the problem. Give the horse a loose rein or put him on light contact. Hit him sharply with the crop behind the girth, and continue to hit him until he goes forward. Be prepared, for the horse may bolt. Even if he does bolt, let him move forward a few strides before you restrain his movement. He is unlikely to run away with you under these circumstances.

BUCKING

Bucking is usually confined to young or to improperly trained horses. However, even old, well-schooled horses may buck at times. When a horse bucks, he humps up his back and leaps forward to land on stiff front legs. Sometimes a horse will tuck his head between his legs and throw his hindquarters about. This kind of bucking is very hard on riders.

A trained horse might buck out of good spirits on a cool morning. It's a good idea to lunge your horse before you ride if he seems unusually frisky.

The horse might buck if he becomes upset. Sometimes a horse will buck if the rider becomes very sloppy and bumps upon his back. This bumping hurts the horse and makes him want to rid himself of the discomfort. Bad fitting tack or improperly adjusted tack can also cause bucking. Horses are very sensitive in the flank. A strap that tightens around his flank will cause any animal to buck. If you use a Western saddle that has a rear cinch, you should tie the cinches together with a short strap to prevent this problem. Horses have been known to throw their riders when the rear cinch slipped into the horse's flank.

If your horse should begin bucking, first secure your seat. If necessary, grab the mane or the saddle. Then shorten your reins. A horse cannot buck very hard if he cannot lower his head. Finally, push your mount forward. He cannot buck and run at the same time. Be careful not to draw your heels up into your horse. This action will make him buck harder. Do not give a bucking horse a loose rein.

After the horse has stopped, and you have caught your breath, try to determine what caused the bucking. Usually there is a definite cause that you can easily correct.

KICKING OUT

Kicking out is sometimes confused with bucking; however, both the action of the horse and the cause of the action are different. Horses sometimes kick out while bucking. Nevertheless, in true kicking out the horse will suddenly throw his hindquarters high in the air and kick out with his hind legs. Poor riders will find themselves catapulted through space. Some-times the horse actually raises his hindquarters above his head.

Horses may kick out at other horses or at dogs. The usual cause of this action is resistance to the crop. The rider will use the crop, and the horse will kick. Some horses will kick when the rider uses the spur, or even when he uses his leg aids too strongly.

Actually, if you have developed your seat to any extent, you will have no difficulty remaining with your horse when he kicks. If necessary, you can brace your hands against his neck.

There are two ways to deal with this problem. You can use the crop upon the shoulder rather than behind the girth; or you can persist in hitting the horse until he yields and goes forward rather than up with his hindquarters. The second method is by far the best. After the horse learns to yield to the crop, he will be less likely to try the kicking trick.

REFUSING TO STAND TO BE MOUNTED

Some horses simply will not stand still while the rider mounts. They will start forward, or back, or swing their quarters to one side. If you have this problem, you should first review the sec-tion in this book on mounting. Perhaps you are making a mis-take and causing the horse's misbehavior. If you are absolutely certain that you are not at fault, then you must take measures to correct the horse.

Many riders punish their horses for moving when they are mounted. You will see riders whip their mounts on the chest, flanks, shoulder, or head. You might see someone grab the bit and jerk. These forms of behavior might make you feel better, but they do your horse nothing but harm.

Remember that horses are creatures of habit. If they move while you mount they are not being purposely bad. They are simply moving because they always move. You must break this bad habit by breaking the pattern of behavior. You must make your horse stand still as you mount; and you must do this enough times to give your horse the habit of standing still, rather than the habit of moving.

You may have someone hold him while you mount. You may tie the horse (leave the halter on under the bridle, and tie with a tie rope). In either case, do not let the horse move until you have taken both stirrups and adjusted the reins. Then move him on a clear command. Don't let him walk because he thought it was a good idea.

If your horse usually stands to be mounted, but moves with you this time, immediately halt. Make the horse stand absolutely still for several seconds. Then move off on a clear command. It is not necessary for you to dismount and try again. Unless you grow careless and sloppy, your horse will not develop this bad habit.

Never whip a horse for moving as you mount. Never jerk the bit! Remember at all times that horses are very simple creatures, and that you must be very patient.

RESISTING BEING BRIDLED

Horses that resist being bridled have had a bad experience somewhere. If your mount throws up his head or refuses the bit, he is not being stubborn. He's trying to avoid a finger in his eye, or a pinched ear, or a bit knocked against his teeth. Since one or two mistakes can turn a gentle horse into one that hates the bridle, you must always be very careful when you put on the bridle.

If your horse does start resisting you, you must use a little psychology. Getting angry and trying to force the bridle will merely make him worse. You must change his mind, and make him think of bridling as a pleasant experience.

To encourage him to open his mouth for the bit, you can rub it with honey. If your horse doesn't like the bridle lifted over his ears, unbuckle the cheek strap on the left of the bridle, and put it on like a halter. When the bridle is safely in place, reward your horse with a little grain. Next, try gently to pull the bridle on the proper way. Reward your horse with a little grain every time he begins to lower his head. Soon he will "have his head in your lap" when you gently pull his ears through the bridle.

Never whip a horse for being hard to bridle. Never try to pry his mouth open, or force the bit into his mouth. Don't try to lower his head by grabbing an ear! Remember, horses are very greedy. They will do almost anything for food. Be gentle with your horse: "You can catch more flies with honey than with vinegar."

EATING WHILE YOU RIDE

Few horses will turn down a tempting morsel of grass if it waves in their face; however, some animals make a habit of dropping their heads without warning to chew upon anything that might be growing under their feet. This habit is caused by greed.

As a general rule, you should not let your horse eat while he is wearing the bridle. Grass will stain the bit and cause green slime to appear in the corners of his mouth. Also, the horse cannot be giving his full attention to his work if he is keeping watch for juicy greenery.

If your mount does grab some grass, you should immediately urge him forward. Use your crop. He cannot eat and hurry forward at the same time.

This is not a habit which can be cured overnight. You must be persistent, and never fail to use the crop when necessary. After a few days, you should have stopped this behavior.

Do not jerk on your mount's mouth, or rein-back. Don't use the crop on his head, or slap him in the mouth with your hand. These actions may cure this habit at the expense of starting worse problems.

ROLLING

All horses like to roll in the dirt. They will roll when they get wet, or when the flies are bothering them, or when they itch. Many horses will roll in water or mud, or in their stalls. This is part of horse behavior. It does not cause a problem unless you happen to be riding the horse at the time.

Once I was riding a little mare through a shallow pond when she began to splash and paw in the water. The next thing I knew she was lying down, and I was covered with mud! I was very embarrassed, since I had a class of students with me at the time.

Before your horse rolls, he will lower his head and begin to sniff the ground. He will probably paw. Certainly, you will feel the front part of his body begin to sink. If this happens, immediately urge him forward! He cannot roll and walk at the same time.

If your horse has been in a stall for a while, you might turn him out a little before you ride. If he has a chance to roll before you mount, he will be less likely to try it with you on his back. Use fly repellent and brush your horse well before you ride in order to prevent itchy skin.

If he tries to roll despite everything, and you find your horse lying on the ground, dismount immediately. Make him rise before he rolls onto your saddle and damages the saddle tree. Then, remount and try again.

STUMBLING

Many times a horse will stumble as he is being ridden. Usually, he will merely catch his toe. Sometimes, he might fall onto his knees. Stumbling most often occurs at the walk, but it can happen at any gait.

The most frequent cause is carelessness by the horse. Your mount will be walking along half asleep and stub his toe against a rock—or he may even fall over his own feet! Horses with big or long feet are particularly prone to this form of clumsiness.

It does no good to punish the horse for stumbling. However, you should check to determine if the cause is more serious than simple carelessness. Your horse may have sore or tender feet that hurt when he hits a stone. He may have a rock in his foot, or be sore in the legs or shoulders. Sometimes, horses have the nerves that lead to their feet severed in an operation to cure navicular disease. After the surgery, they have no feeling in their hooves, and are likely to stumble. Have your horse checked by a veterinarian. If he can find no problems, you can assume your horse is merely clumsy.

Moderate clumsiness is merely an aggravation; more frequent stumbling can be dangerous. If your horse is very clumsy you might consider getting a more sure-footed mount.

PULLING OVER THE BIT, GETTING BEHIND THE BIT, AND HEAD-TOSSING

Pulling Over the Bit

All three of these problems can be caused by severe or annoying bits, by heavy hands, or by a weak seat.

A horse which is over the bit may be pulling against the rider's hands, or he may hold his head so far upwards that his nose points towards the sky (stargazing).

A pulling horse is constantly fighting his rider. He pushes firmly against the bit. Sometimes he even jerks forward in an attempt to pull the reins from the rider's hands. You should avoid taking lessons on a horse which pulls. If your animal begins to pull during your lessons, you must try to determine what is causing the difficulty. Chances are good that your problem is being caused by heavy, jerking hands. Try riding off contact until your hands improve.

Stargazing is also caused by poor hands, or by severe bits

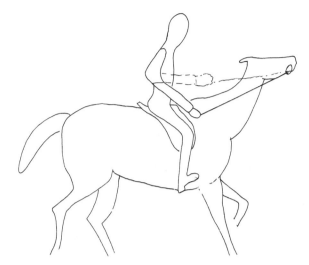

Figure 8–3. Stargazing (over the bit): Poor, heavy hands attempt to pull the horse's head down. Actually, they make him raise his head higher. You can correct this problem by raising your hands until there is a straight line from your elbow to the horse's mouth. After a few minutes, the horse will lower his head.

(see Figure 8-3). The horse holds his head so that your hands cannot hurt him. If your horse begins to stargaze, you should check your bit. Maybe you need to adjust it in his mouth, or to change to something less severe. By all means work to improve your hands by riding off contact for a while. A standing martingale can serve as a crutch to help you until you improve your riding skills.

Getting Behind the Bit

Some horses react to heavy hands or severe bits by getting behind the bit (see Figure 8-4). Here the animal tucks his chin until his head is behind the vertical. He bends his neck behind the poll. The result is loss of control by the rider. In fact, a horse can become chronic in this habit, and thus be ruined for most work. You should avoid taking lessons on a horse which goes behind the bit. If your gentle lesson horse begins this trait, you can be sure that either the bit or your riding is at fault. Immediately switch to a mild bit. You should ride on a loose rein most of the time while you strengthen your seat and legs. The only cure is a combination of light rein aids and strong seat and leg aids. You must push your horse forward so that he does not go behind the bit.

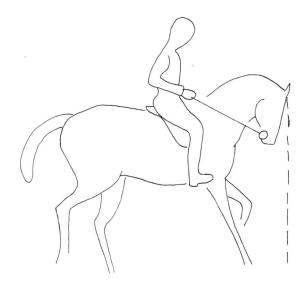

Figure 8–4. Overflexion (behind the bit): Heavy, pulling hands and weak legs can cause the horse to overflex his neck. His head is held behind the vertical. The rider should soften his hands and push the horse with his seat and legs.

Head-Tossing

Head-tossing is probably caused by some aggravation to the horse. Some horses will toss their heads if the bit or the rider's hands are too severe. Frequently the cause is a fly on the animal's face, or a bit adjusted too low in his mouth. If your horse begins to toss his head, check the adjustment of your bridle. Use fly repellent on his face before you ride. Finally, lighten your hands and use stronger seat and leg aids. If you cannot correct his head tossing, consult a veterinarian. Your horse might have some infection or tooth trouble that you cannot see. One note: A martingale will not correct head-tossing. If your martingale is so tight that it restricts head-tossing, it is too tight.

JIGGING

Sometimes you will find a horse which jigs and dances rather than going at a calm, even pace. He will break into the trot from the walk at every other step. If you attempt to hold him back, he will either prance or rear. Meanwhile, you are having a very uncomfortable ride.

271

Horses jig and prance because of poor early training. If they are not taught to walk calmly on a loose rein at the start of their schooling, they tend to think they should always go full speed. A well-trained horse may jig if he is impatient or upset.

If your horse begins to jig, you should bring him to a full stop. Make him stand quietly and calm him with your voice. Pats upon his neck are very relaxing to the horse. If you cannot halt, circle and try again. In general, the halt is the only cure for jigging—that, and careful retraining to teach your horse to move calmly on a loose rein. Remember, always walk more than you trot, and trot more than you canter. You will not only protect your horse's legs and wind, but you will also keep him from thinking that he must rush forward.

Sometimes you must halt again and again before your horse will walk calmly. Do not get angry and jerk the reins or hit your mount. Be patient. After only a few such sessions, you will have corrected the problem forever.

Never buy a horse that cannot walk calmly on a loose rein.

CUTTING CORNERS

Cutting the corners in the ring is an annoying habit of school horses. The animal will gradually take a smaller and smaller track around the ring. Naturally, he wants to do as little work as possible—and going into the corners is more work than cutting around. The cause is initially weak riding. Later, the horse can become confirmed in this habit, so that even strong riders take him into the corners with difficulty.

If your horse tends to cut corners, you should do your best to correct him. Never ride sloppily through the corners of the ring. It might help you to place barrels, jump standards, or bending poles in the corners just to the inside of the track (see Figure 8-5). You should always ride to the outside of the poles.

To push your horse into the corners, follow these steps (see Figure 8-6):

1. Prepare for the corner by gathering your reins and pressing your seat into the saddle.

2. On the turn, use your inside leg behind the girth! If necessary, use the crop on the inside behind the girth.

3. On the turn, your inside rein should be used indirectly, or you should use the inside neck rein. The outside rein should keep the horse from overbending his neck to the inside.

4. As soon as your horse goes well into the corner, switch your hands and legs to the normal aids for the turn and ride him out of the turn smoothly.

Figure 8–5. Barrels as a correction for corner cutting.

Figure 8–6. Aids to push the horse into the corners.

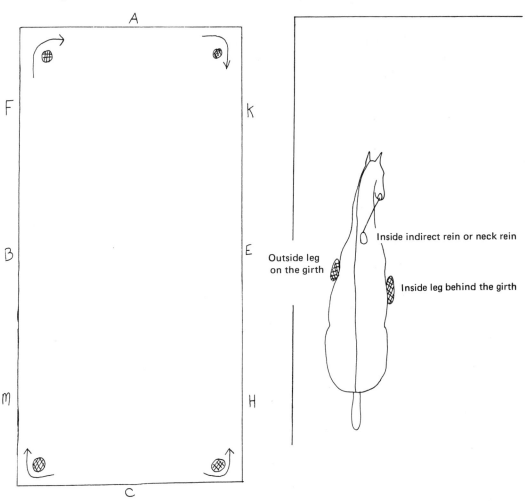

REFUSALS, RUNOUTS, AND RUSHING

These are three problems you might have while jumping. All three are initially caused by poor riding and poor judgment. After a while, they can become habits which are very difficult to cure.

Refusals

When a horse refuses, he will trot or canter nearly to a jump, only to stop at the last minute. Sometimes horses actually fall into a jump. Any horse might refuse at times. He might come into the jump wrong, so that he knows he cannot take the jump without accident. Or he might think the jump is too large for his abilities. If a horse refuses frequently, however, it is probably due to one or more of the following: The animal has sore feet or sore legs; the rider is jerking his mouth or falling onto his back over the jump; the rider is not pushing the horse into the jump; the jumps have been raised too high for the horse at this stage of his training.

Lower the jumps; check your form (grab the mane and stay out of the saddle until after your mount lands!); and be sure to ride your horse strongly into the jumps (see Figure 8-7). If you

Figure 8–7. Cure for refusals.

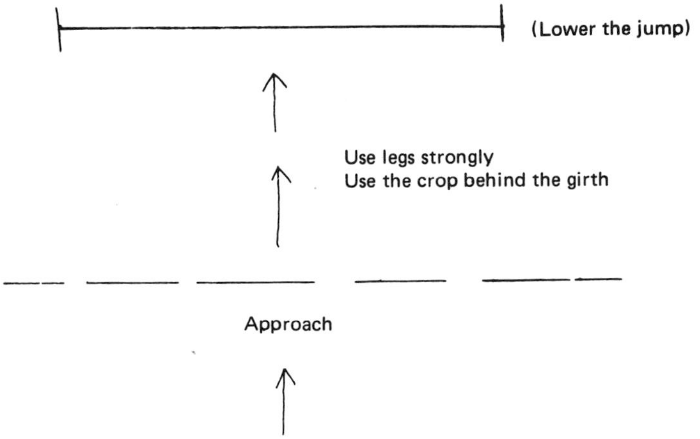

(Lower the jump)

Use legs strongly
Use the crop behind the girth

Approach

still have problems with refusals, consult your veterinarian. Your horse might have soreness which hurts him when he jumps.

Runouts

In a runout, the horse will approach the jump, only to duck out to one side at the last minute. Runouts are caused by the same factors as refusals. An additional cause of runouts is jumps that are too narrow (for a cure, see Figure 8-8).

Figure 8–8. Cure for runouts.

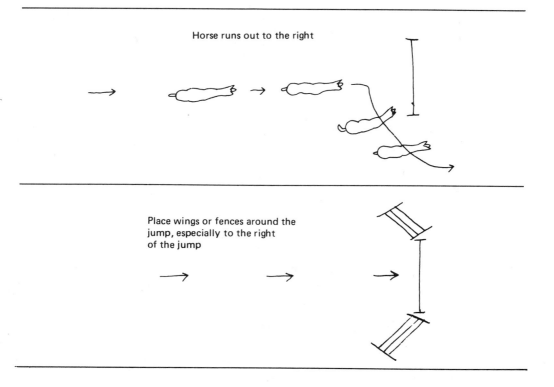

If your horse is running out, lower your jumps, check your form, and be sure to ride your horse strongly into the jumps. It might help to place wings, or extensions, on each side of the jump to make the obstacle wider. You will notice that the horse usually tries to run out to the same side. To counter this, you may place the jump along a fence. Carry the crop on that side, at any rate. When the horse begins to run out, pop him firmly behind the girth several times. Let him know you are not pleased with his actions, but do not lose your temper.

Rushing

You may be able to make your horse take a jump even if your form over the jump is very bad. In this case, strong riding will drive him into the jump; and then harsh hands will jerk his mouth over the jump. The horse will react by beginning to rush. A rushing horse speeds before a jump. He throws up his head and approaches at a full gallop. The poor rider has no control at all.

If your horse begins to rush, lower your jumps, and check your form (see Figure 8-9 for cures). Be absolutely certain you are not jerking him over the jump. Many people come down in the saddle too soon, without realizing it! Stay out of the saddle until after your horse lands! To specifically counter rushing, practice jumping from the trot. If your horse begins to rush, circle him before the jump and approach again. Cavaletti work is also good for rushers. After each jump, make your horse walk calmly on a loose rein. This may take some time at first. Eventually, however, you should be able to calm your horse immediately after each jump.

As with all jumping problems, have the veterinarian check your horse for soreness. I've known many horses that hated jumping because they had sore feet.

Of course, we all hope that you will never have any trouble with your horse. Life would be ideal if horses always understood

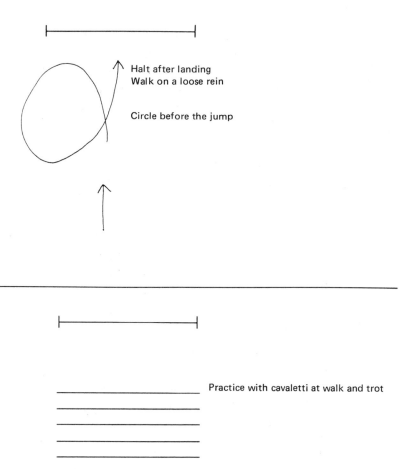

Halt after landing
Walk on a loose rein

Circle before the jump

Practice with cavaletti at walk and trot

Figure 8–9. Cures for rushing.

their riders, and if the animals always did as they were told. Unfortunately, life is not ideal, and horses do sometimes misunderstand, or deliberately misbehave. You should have picked up enough advice from this chapter to help you cope with these discipline and communication problems when they do occur. The more experience you have with riding, and with horses, the fewer difficulties you will have in controlling your mount.

To learn to ride well takes many hours in the saddle. When you finish all the lessons and exercises in this book, you should be a fair rider. You should have a secure seat in the saddle, and know enough about riding to be able to ride trails, show in beginner classes, jump low obstacles, or compete in simple Western games. Where you go from here is entirely up to you.

Perhaps you have no further ambitions. You are happy knowing no more about riding than you do now. This is fine. You know enough to be a safe rider, and to enjoy your horse without harm to yourself or to your mount.

If you want to learn to ride better, however, you can look forward to many more hours of careful practice. These hours need not be hours of drudgery. I hope that you enjoyed the Lessons in this book. I know you will enjoy the hours you must dedicate practicing in order to improve your riding. You need not practice by riding around and around in the ring. You can practice on the trails and fields. You can show and compete, gaining both experience and an expert judgment of your skills given by a competent horse show judge. Practically any experience in the saddle will help you to become a bolder and more talented horseman or horsewoman.

Riding is one of the most complex of all sports. It is also, I think, one of the most enjoyable sports. Once you learn the basics of horsemanship, you can have equal fun trail riding with your friends, or preparing for serious mounted competition. I have loved riding from the first time I sat on a horse, and my experiences with my horses are some of the most valued in my life. I hope that in future years you will be able to say the same. For now, I wish you happy riding! Have fun on your horse.

Appendix: Test Answers

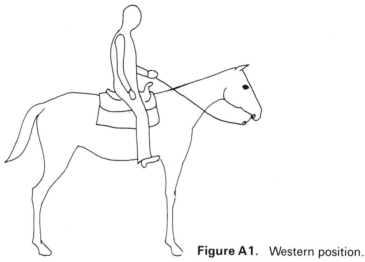

Figure A1. Western position.

Figure A2a. Position at the walk, halt, and sitting trot.

Figure A2b. Posting trot, rising position.

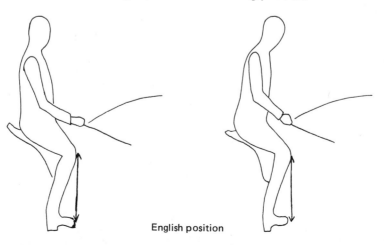

English position

PART I, CHAPTERS 1–2

1. *See* Figure 1–1.
2. *See* pp. 8–9.
3. *See* Figure 1–2.
4. *See* Figure 1–3.
5. *See* pp. 38–39.

PART II, CHAPTERS 3–5

1. True or False (True = +   False = −)
   a.   +
   b.   −
   c.   +
   d.   +
   e.   −
   f.   −
   g.   −
2. Safety rules for tying your horse:
   a.   Never tie by the lead strap.
   b.   Never tie by the reins, or by a rope snapped to the bit.
   c.   Tie to something solid.
   d.   Don't give too much slack, and don't tie the rope too low.
   e.   Don't leave your horse tied and unattended.
   f.   Don't tie your horse out to graze.
3. Grooming your horse before riding:
   a.   Brush with a dandy brush.
   b.   Dress wounds and lumps
   c.   Clean the animal's hooves.

4. Multiple choice
   a. (2)
   b. (3)
   c. (3)
   d. (3)

5. Describe the cure for each of the following problems:
   a. *Kicking:* Say "No!" firmly, and slap your horse on the hip with your hand.
   b. *Nipping:* Say "No!" and slap your horse on the chest.
   c. *Stepping on your feet:* Do not punish your horse. Try to keep your feet out of his way.
   d. *Eating wood:* Paint creosote on the boards.
   e. *Being hard to catch in the pasture:* Keep your horse by himself, and take feed to him when you go to catch him. Leave a halter on him if necessary.

6. Nine rules to follow in coping with problems with your horse:
   a. Never hit your horse on the head.
   b. Never scream.
   c. Never beat your horse with a whip.
   d. Never lose your temper.
   e. Never panic.
   f. Never chase your horse.
   g. Never allow your horse to chase you.
   h. Never wave strange objects that might frighten your horse.
   i. If you do punish your horse, do it immediately after the infraction.

PART III, CHAPTER 6, LESSONS 1–4A

1. Define the following terms:
    a. *See* p. 107.
    b. *See* p. 101.
    c. *See* p. 104.
    d. *See* pp. 108–110.
    e. *See* p. 113.
    f. *See* pp. 115–118.
    g. *See* p. 119.
    h. *See* p. 120.
    i. *See* p. 120.
    j. *See* p. 123.

2. True or false

a.	—	k.	+	u.	—
b.	+	l.	—	v.	+
c.	+	m.	—	w.	—
d.	—	n.	+	x.	+
e.	—	o.	+	y.	—
f.	—	p.	—		
g.	+	q.	+		
h.	—	r.	—		
i.	—	s.	+		
j.	+	t.	—		

PART III, CHAPTER 7, LESSONS 5–8

1. True or false

a.	+	e.	+	i.	—
b.	—	f.	+	j.	+
c.	+	g.	—	k.	+
d.	+	h.	—	l.	+

m.	−	t.	+
n.	−	u.	+
o.	−	v.	−
p.	+	w.	+
q.	+	x.	+
r.	−	y.	−
s.	−		

2. Define the following terms:

   a. *See* p. 135.

   b. *See* pp. 144–147.

   c. *See* pp. 147–151.

   d. *See* p. 152.

   e. *See* pp. 153.

PART III, CHAPTER 7, LESSONS 9–12

1. True or false

a.	+	i.	+	q.	+
b.	+	j.	−	r.	+
c.	−	k.	+	s.	−
d.	−	l.	−	t.	+
e.	+	m.	−	u.	−
f.	+	n.	+	v.	−
g.	−	o.	−	w.	−
h.	+	p.	−	x.	−

2. Find these terms in the text.

   a. *See* pp. 178–180.

   b. *See* pp. 180–183.

   c. *See* p. 183.

   d. *See* pp. 192–194.

   e. *See* pp. 195–197.

FINAL EXAM: WRITTEN TESTS

1. True or false

a. +	k. +	u. +
b. −	l. +	v. +
c. −	m. −	w. −
d. +	n. −	x. +
e. −	o. −	y. +
f. −	p. −	
g. −	q. +	
h. −	r. −	
i. −	s. −	
j. −	t. −	

2. Multiple choice

a. (2)	i. (1)	q. (3)
b. (3)	j. (3)	r. (1)
c. (2)	k. (2)	s. (2)
d. (1)	l. (3)	t. (2)
e. (2)	m. (1)	u. (2)
f. (1)	n. (2)	v. (3)
g. (3)	o. (3)	w. (2)
h. (2)	p. (3)	x. (1)
		y. (3)

3. Definitions:

   a. *Pommel:* The front portion of the saddle. It is in front of the rider and over the horse's withers.

   b. *Leading rein:* A simple rein effect. The rider pulls his hand out in the direction of movement, leading the horse into the turn.

   c. *Crop:* A short whip.

   d. *Leg behind the girth:* The rider's leg (calf and heel) is applied to the horse one to ten inches behind the girth of the saddle.

e. *Neck-rein:* The rein is applied to the horse's neck so that the horse moves away from the rein. The rider also uses his seat and legs on the turn. The horse looks away from the direction of movement. In a correct turn, the horse will neither speed nor slow his gait.

f. *Skidding:* The haunches of the horse do not follow his shoulders. Instead, they slide outwards so that the horse moves around the turn at an angle.

g. *On contact:* The rider is on contact with the horse's mouth through the reins. There should be a straight line from the rider's elbow to the horse's mouth. Correctly, the rider should maintain the same degree of contact at all times. He should not allow the reins to slacken and tighten with the horse's strides. He shouldn't need to gather the reins to slow his gait.

h. *Good hands:* The rider's hands are quiet, and do not jerk on the horse's mouth. The hands are light, not heavy or pulling. They respond to the horse. They guide and direct; they do not pull or yank.

i. *Direct rein:* The rein effect which acts directly upon the horse's mouth. The rider tightens the rein by moving his hand slightly backwards and to the side. The horse should respond by yielding with his mouth, lowering his head slightly in the direction of movement, and turning his head so that the rider can see the horse's eye.

j. *Indirect rein:* The rein effect which acts indirectly upon the horse's mouth. The rider tightens the rein so that it presses against the horse's neck. The rider's hand does not cross over the horse's neck. Used alone, the indirect rein causes the horse to turn away from the action of the rein.

Used with the direct rein, this rein effect keeps the horse from over-bending his neck in the direction of movement.

k. *Curb:* A bit which has a curb chain. Usually this bit has a ported mouth (a ''hill'' in the mouth) and long shanks (the shanks lead from the mouth to the reins). Curb bits act upon the horse's jaw rather than simply upon his mouth.

l. *Fixed hands:* The rider closes his hands upon the reins and fixes them in place so that they do not give the reins to the horse. Fixed hands restrict; they do not pull.

m. *Pivot leg:* In a half-turn on the forehand, the horse pivots, or turns around, the inside foreleg. This leg remains in place.

n. *To ride a straight line:* The horse will move along a line as straight as one drawn with a straight-edge. His hind legs will follow his forelegs at all times. He will not waver, skid, hesitate, or speed his gait.

o. *Change of hand:* A change of direction. In the half-circle and half-circle in reverse, the change of hand occurs at the transition from the semi-circle to the diagonal to the track. At this point, the rider changes hand and leg aids.

p. *The rider's aids:* Aids help in controlling and directing the horse. The natural aids are the rider's hands, seat, legs, and weight. The crop and spurs are artificial aids.

q. *Period of suspension:* At various gaits and movements, the horse is temporarily suspended in the air with all four legs off the ground. This occurs at the trot, the gallop or canter, and the jump. It does not occur in the walk.

r. *Vibrating the reins:* The rider opens and closes

his hands, or otherwise causes the reins to quiver softly. This action increases the sensitivity of the horse to the bit.

s. *Haunches:* The horse's hindquarters, including everything to the rear of the rider.

t. *To range the haunches:* The horse throws his haunches out to one side, so that he is not moving on a straight line. Usually this is a bad fault that should be corrected by proper use of the rider's leg and seat aids.

u. *Following action of the rider:* The rider follows the horse's mouth with his hands, so that he maintains even contact with the horse's mouth at all times.

v. *School figures:* Ways of riding in the ring which develop the skill of the rider and the responsiveness of the horse. These include the circle, the half-circle, the turn across the ring, the small circle, the half-circle in reverse, the figure eight, the diagonal, the serpentine, the broken line, and others.

w. *Canter depart:* The moment when the horse strikes off into the canter. Departs may be from the walk or the trot. The horse should begin to canter smoothly, without speeding his gait or hesitating. He should take the requested lead.

x. *Simple lead change:* The change from one canter lead to the other through several strides of the walk or the trot.

y. *Hand-gallop:* The horse gallops under full control of the rider. He is on firm contact. The rider is forward, out of the saddle, with his hands well down the horse's neck.

Glossary

ABOVE THE BIT: The horse pushes his head forward until the bit no longer acts in the proper place in his mouth. Such a horse is evading the action of the bit, and trying to escape the commands of the rider's hands.

BACKING: The horse steps backwards. This is also, and more correctly, called the rein-back.

BARN SOUR: A bad habit where the horse refuses to leave the barn, or tries to return to the barn.

BEARING REIN: This is also called the neck-rein. The rein is pushed against the upper portion of the horse's neck, causing him to move away from the rein.

BEHIND THE BIT: The horse pulls his head towards his body until the bit no longer acts in the proper place in his mouth. Such a horse is evading the action of the bit, and trying to escape the commands of the rider.

BEHIND THE GIRTH: An area on the horse's side directly behind the girth or cinch of the saddle, where the rider applies his legs to give aids and commands to the horse.

BOARDING STABLE: A stable where horse owners may keep their horses for a fee.

BODY BRUSH: A soft grooming brush used to polish the horse's coat and to brush his face.

BOSAL: A device used in place of a bit in training many Western horses. The bosal fits around the nose and acts by pressing on the soft cartilage of the nose.

BRADOON: A small snaffle bit designed to be used with a curb bit in a full, or Weymouth, bridle.

BREECHES: English riding pants, worn with knee-high boots.

BUCK KNEES: The knees bend forward. These are weak knees.

CALF KNEES: The knees bend backwards. These knees are strong. However, a calf-kneed horse tends to have rough, choppy gaits.

CANTER: A slow, controlled gallop.

CANTER DEPART: The first stride of the canter, when the horse changes from a walk or a trot to a canter.

COLT: A stallion or gelding less than five years old.

COOLER: A light-weight cover that is placed over a hot horse to keep him from getting chilled while he cools.

CROP: A short whip carried by the rider and used to help control the horse.

CROSS-TIE: A device for restraining the horse. The horse is tied with two ropes, one on each side of his halter. These ropes attach to poles, or rings on a wall some distance from the horse on each side. The ropes stretch from his head to the rings in straight lines parallel to the ground. The horse is thus restricted in his movements, and cannot pin his groom against the wall.

CURB: A bit that gives added control with a lever action on the horse's jaw. Curbs usually have ported (humped) mouth pieces, shanks going from the mouth piece to the reins, and a curb chain or strap.

CURB CHAIN, OR STRAP: A chain or leather strap that goes from one side of the curb bit to the other, fitting snugly under the horse's chin. This chain is necessary in order for the lever action of the curb bit to be effective.

CURRY COMB: A rubber or metal grooming tool. It is used to clean the grooming brushes, and to remove dirt and loose hair from the horse's coat.

DANDY BRUSH: A stiff brush used in grooming the horse to remove dust and dirt.

DIRECT REIN EFFECT: The rider uses the rein directly backwards, so that the rein acts in a straight line from the horse's mouth to the rider's elbow. This rein effect can be used to halt or turn the horse.

DRAFT HORSE: A horse of a breed developed for farm work and heavy labor. These animals are large, heavy, and sluggish. Some draft breeds are: Shire, Belgian, Percheron, Clydesdale, and Suffock Punch.

DROPPED NOSEBAND: A noseband on a bridle that is dropped down to just above or just below the bit, and tightened so that the horse cannot throw open his mouth to evade the bit. Dropped nosebands should only be used with snaffle bits.

DROP WEIGHT IN SADDLE: The rider braces his back and pushes his weight down into the saddle.

ELEMENTARY DRESSAGE: This is a system of riding that includes school figures and other exercises discussed in this manual. Elementary dressage tests are given in special shows, and the horses and riders are judged according to the skills they display.

EWE NECK: The horse's neck is concave along its top line. Some horses have ewe necks at birth. Others are given ewe necks by severe bits and bad riding.

FEEL: The rider should develop his ability to feel what his horse is doing. He should be able to tell which diagonal he is on in posting, and which lead the horse is on in cantering, by the way the horse feels. The "feel" of the horse is transmitted to the rider through his seat, legs, and hands.

FILLY: A mare less than five years old.

FIXED HANDS: The rider fixes his hands in place, in the air, so that they no longer follow the action of the horse's head and neck. Fixed hands are stationary in space. They are not pulled backwards, or set against the horse's neck.

FLEX IN THE JAW: The horse relaxes his jaw and chews on the bit. He does not open his mouth wide. The reins will feel soft in the rider's hands. All well-trained horses should flex in the jaw, rather than pull or go behind the bit.

FLEX IN THE POLL: The horse bends his neck in the poll, so that his face becomes vertical to the ground. Flexion in the poll is part of advanced horsemanship. Only an experienced rider can flex a horse in the poll without causing him to over-flex, or go behind the bit.

FOLLOWING ACTION OF THE HANDS: The rider's hands should always keep a steady contact on the reins. In order to do this, they must move with the horse's head and neck at the walk and the canter.

GAIT: A way of moving for the horse. The natural gaits for most horses are the walk, trot, and gallop. Some horses have other natural gaits, or artificial gaits that are taught to them by a trainer.

GALLOP: A three-beat gait, faster than the walk or the trot.

GALLOPING POSITION: The position the rider should take while riding the gallop. He leans forward from his knees, standing in the stirrups. He places his hands on the horse's neck after shortening the reins to remain on contact. Western riders also stand in the stirrups and lean forward.

GELDING: A castrated male horse. Most male horses are gelded, since geldings make excellent riding animals. The majority of stallions are difficult to manage and are used only for breeding. Some stallions are ridden, but they take much more skill and are much more difficult to control than are geldings.

GIRTH SORES: Sores under the girth or cinch are called girth sores. These wounds are caused by the rubbing and chafing action of the girth. They are difficult to cure, but can be prevented by careful saddling, and by keeping girths and cinches clean and soft.

HACKAMORE: Used in place of a bit, this device works by applying pressure on the soft cartilage of the horse's nose.

HACK STABLE: A stable that rents horses by the hour or by the month.

HAND: A measure of height in horses. One hand equals four inches.

HAND-GALLOP: A gallop where the rider takes the galloping position and keeps the horse firmly on contact. The speed of the hand-gallop is about 18 miles per hour.

HARNESS HORSE: Any horse that is trained to pull a cart. Some breeds were developed especially for harness work; among these are Standardbreds, Hackneys, and Hackney Ponies.

HEAD SHY: The horse is afraid to have his head touched, and holds it up and away from the groom.

HOOF PICK: A grooming tool used to clean the undersides of horse's hooves of dirt and stones.

HUNT BOOTS: Knee-high boots, worn with breeches.

HUNT CAP: A velvet-covered hard hat worn for the rider's protection.

HUNTER: Any horse shown in Hunter classes at horse shows, or used in the field on fox hunts. Hunters frequently have at least some thoroughbred breeding. They should be pleasant to ride, travel at all gaits on light contact, and jump smoothly over a variety of obstacles.

HUNTSEAT: A style of riding developed for fox hunting and show jumping.

IMPULSION: The willingness to move forward. A horse is said to have impulsion when he is balanced under his rider and will go forward freely to the rider's aids.

IN-AND-OUT: This type of obstacle on a jump course consists of two jumps. The horse jumps over one jump, takes one canter stride, and jumps over the second jump.

INDIRECT REIN EFFECT: The rider pushes one rein against the horse's neck, just above the withers. The horse moves away from the rein.

IN FRONT OF THE GIRTH: The rider uses his leg on the horse directly to the front of the girth or cinch of the saddle.

JIGGING: The horse prances, refusing to do a calm, flat-footed walk.

JODHPURS: Long English-style riding pants, usually worn with short jodhpur boots.

JUMPS: Obstacles designed to be jumped by horses. They usually consist of upright standards, horizontal jump rails, and special cups which attach to the standards and support the rails.

JUMP COURSE: A series of jumps. Courses are designed to be taken by the horse and rider in a pre-determined sequence.

JUMPER: Any horse shown in jumper classes in horse shows. A jumper may be of any breed. He is trained to go over a variety of high and wide obstacles in a limited period of time. Jumpers are frequently very high-strung because of the highly competitive nature of their work.

KIMBERWICKE: This bit is a combination of a curb and a snaffle. It has a ported mouth and a curb chain, with D-shaped snaffle rings. The kimberwicke is a good bit for many horses, since it gives more control than a snaffle, yet it is not very severe.

LEADING REIN EFFECT: The rider moves his hand and rein out to the side and leads his horse into the turn.

LEAD STRAP: A leather or cloth strap with a chain on one end, designed for leading a horse.

LUNGING: A way of training and exercising the horse while dismounted. The trainer stands in the middle of a circle while the horse walks or trots around him.

MANE COMB: A grooming tool, used for pulling the mane and tail. Most grooms do not regularly comb the mane and tail, as combing tends to split the hairs.

MARE: A female horse.

NEAR: The horseman's term for left, as in the left side of the horse and the saddle. The opposite of near is off.

NECK-REIN: The common term for the bearing rein.

OFF: Horseman's word for right, as the right side of the horse and saddle. The opposite of off is near.

ON THE GIRTH: The rider uses his leg on the girth when he squeezes or taps directly over the girth or the cinch of the saddle.

OVERFLEXION: The horse bends his head towards his body in an attempt to evade the bit—also called "behind the bit."

PARK HORSE: Any horse trained for park classes at horse shows. Park horses may be of any breed, but are most frequently American Saddlebreds, Morgans, or Arabians. These horses are ridden saddleseat style. They are judged on the beauty of their movements and on their behavior in the show ring.

PELHAM: A bit that combines a curb and a snaffle in one bit. It has only one mouth piece, but is used with two sets of reins. Pelhams are more severe than snaffles or kimberwickes.

POINTS OF THE BUTTOCKS: The two little bones each of us has under the most fleshy portion of the seat.

PONY: Any horse 14.2 hands or less in height at the withers. A pony may be a small horse, or he may be an individual from a special pony breed. Some pony breeds are Welsh, Shetland, Connemara, Hackney pony, and Pony of America (POA).

PUSH WITH YOUR SEAT: The rider stiffens his back so that the points of the buttocks are pressed down into the saddle.

RACE HORSE: A horse that competes in races against other horses for prizes. Race horses are usually Thoroughbreds, Quarter Horses, or Standardbreds. The horses race on flat tracks or over jumps; horses that race over jumps are called steeplechasers.

RANGED HAUNCHES: The horse travels with his haunches or hindquarters out to one side so that his hind feet do not travel in the tracks of his fore feet.

REVERSE THROUGH THE RING: The rider travels across the ring, changing his direction of movement on the track when he reaches the other side.

SADDLE SEAT: A style of riding developed for riding park horses. The saddle is very flat, and the bridle usually has both a curb bit and a bradoon. American Saddlebreds, Arabians, Morgans, and Tennessee Walking horses are some breeds frequently shown saddle seat.

SADDLE SORES: Sores under the saddle. They may be caused by rubbing, pressure, or heat.

SCHOOLING HELMET: Basically, a hunt cap that is not covered with velvet. It is designed to protect the rider's head in case of a fall.

SKIDDING: A horse may skid with his hind feet on a turn, just like a motorcycle can skid on its back wheel on a turn. Skidding is not a good habit in horses. Riders should try to avoid skidding around turns.

SNAFFLE: A very mild bit, consisting of a jointed mouth piece and two rings for the attachment of the reins.

SPREAD JUMP: Any jump that is wide as well as high.

STALLION: A male horse.

STEEPLECHASER: A horse that races against other horses over a track with jumps.

STIRRUP BAR: On an English saddle, the stirrup bar is a metal bar that serves to attach the leathers to the saddle.

STOCK SEAT: A rider in stock seat uses a Western saddle and a curb bit. This style of riding was developed in the United States for herding cattle. It is very popular now for pleasure riding as well as for games and rodeos.

SWEAT SCRAPER: A grooming tool, used to remove excess water from the horse's coat. It is usually a piece of curved aluminum.

TACK: Any device used on the horse in riding.

TIE ROPE: A sturdy rope used to tie the horse. A tie rope is the only proper rope or strap used in tying. A horse should never be tied by the reins or the lead strap.

TRIPLE JUMP: A triple is like an in-and-out, but has three jumps in the series rather than two.

TROT: A two-beat gait. The horse's legs act in diagonal pairs.

VICE: An incurable, bad habit.

WALK: A four-beat gait. Each hoof strikes the ground individually. The walk is fairly slow.

WAVERING: The horse is said to waver when he does not move in a straight line. He steps first to one side of the straight line, and then to the other. Green horses will not travel in straight lines. Also, green riders allow their horses to waver.

WESTERN HORSE: Any horse ridden with Western equipment. Certain breeds are more frequently ridden Western than other breeds. Some of these breeds are Quarter Horses, Appaloosas, and Paints. Almost any horse may be ridden Western or English, depending upon the desires of the rider, and upon the horse's training.

Index